Stay in the Game

By Rena Beadle

Stay in the Game

Copyright ©2009, 2014
By Rena Beadle
Stayinthegameministries.com

Published by:
SpiriTruth Publishing Co.
7710-T Cherry Park Dr, Ste 224
Houston, Texas 77095
www.SpiriTruthPublishing.com

Scripture quotations taken from the New Living Translation,

Scripture quotations taken from the Message Bible

ISBN 978-1-304-90849-0

Printed in the United States of America

All rights reserved.

No part of this publication may be reproduced, stored in a retrieval system or transmitted in any form or by any means - electronic, mechanical, digital photocopy, recording, or any other without the prior written permission of the author.

Dedication

To my Heavenly Father who makes all things new and the six greatest men in my game:

Leo, Jon, David, Chris, Jeremy and Michael Beadle

ACKNOWLEDGEMENTS AND THANKS TO:

Eddie Smith, for his writing seminar and invaluable coaching throughout the writing process. I could not have written this book without him and will always be forever grateful.

Kim Dyer, Krystal Williams, Lynda Pringle, Crystal Comeaux and Liz White for their suggestions, input and constant encouragement.

The Entire Beadle Family, beginning with Grandpa and Grandma Beadle, for being the most loving and fun filled family in the world.

Mark Magbee, for being the greatest brother, brother-in-law and uncle to me, Leo and five rambunctious nephews.

Holly Pointer, my cousin, for helping me stay in the game when I wanted to quit.

The Timmerman family, for always staying in the game.

Kathy Hyde, my friend who continues to stay in the game no matter what.

The Hyche family, for encouraging us each step of the way.

Gary and Pam Babineaux, our mentors and friends who taught us how to stay in the game.

Victory Worship Center for believing in us.

Pastors Joel and Victoria Osteen, for teaching us how to courageously step through doors of opportunity.

Lakewood Church's Worship Leaders for always walking in faith and integrity.

Graham Cooke, for his prophetic teachings that taught us how kind God truly is.

The Beadle Men, for adding to the chapters of the book. Stay in the Game will always serve as a reminder of God's faithfulness for many generations to come.

Table of Contents

Chapter 1 - Reality *Show, Courtship and Marriage*.......*page 9*

Chapter 2 - *Self-Employed -- Yikes!*...............................*page 27*

Chapter 3 - *Shattered Dreams*..*page 39*

Chapter 4 - *Remaining a Family*....................................*page 51*

Chapter 5 - *Faith vs. Stupidity!*......................................*page 63*

Chapter 6 - *Get Up!*..*page 77*

Chapter 7 - *Springs In the Desert*..................................*page 93*

Chapter 8 - *New Beginnings*..*page 105*

Chapter 9 - *Back to Basics*...*page 119*

Chapter 10 - *Treated Like Royalty*................................*page 131*

Chapter 11 - *Stay in the Game*......................................*page 145*

Chapter 12 - *Moving Forward*......................................*page 153*

APPENDIX...*page 163*

Foreword

We must see our lives as both a story and a journey. The Bible is the story of people who have an encounter with God and are empowered to turn it into an ongoing experience of His Nature. In the process of abiding with us and walking out our life situations, the Father makes us into His image.

The story of Rena and her family is the potential story for each of us. It is the journey of discovering what God is really, really like! It is the story of restoration, revelation, and the surprise experiences of a Father who is unique in His loving-kindness to each of us. As we journey with Rena we learn to see life through the eyes of God's goodness.

What we behold is what we become.

Graham Cooke

Chapter 1

Reality Show, Courtship and Marriage

"Hello. What? We are your favorite family? What's next?" A few days earlier, my sons and I drove to a mall in Katy, Texas to audition for Americas Busiest Family reality show. My husband, Leo, was out of town on business. "Honey, we made the first audition." "How?" he replied. "I don't know, but get ready! They are sending a producer over to meet you. They want a 10 minute video of us, sharing how busy we are, as well as any music we can perform." Never in a million years would I have thought we would be auditioning for a reality show, let alone being chosen to participate.

It was February of 2005. I was working for a community newspaper, when a reporter came to me with an NBC press release. "Rena, we just received information concerning a reality show, called America's Busiest Family. You are the busiest lady I know. You have five boys, and a full time job. You are what they are looking for." I listened to him in disbelief as he rambled on and on about how there was a big cash prize and it would be worth it to at least check it out. "Do you want cameras to follow us around our apartment all the time?" Leo moaned. I had to think of a quick response. "What would Pastor Joel say?" I asked. I knew I had asked the right question. We attend Lakewood church in Houston, Texas, where Joel and Victoria Osteen pastor. He is always preaching about how when opportunity knocks, open the door. Our apartment was small for seven people. I wondered how many cameras there would be… Finally, Leo agreed. "We probably won't be chosen, but go ahead and try."

On a cold winter night, I piled the kids in the suburban and headed towards Katy, Texas. I called a friend of mine to get directions because the traffic was horrible that evening. As I told her what we were going to do, she said, "Rena, I have a very good feeling about this audition. I feel God's hand is in the middle of this." She then directed me to the mall where NBC was situated. We were almost late as we ran into the food court hoping we had not missed our opportunity.

The sign pointed to the Katy Mall food court. As we ran over to NBC's booth, my wedding band flew off my finger just in time to meet one of the producers. She looked at me, then at the floor, and said, "Ma'am is that your wedding ring?" I laughed and said, "It sure is." I quickly became comfortable as we giggled over my mishap. She pointed to some nearby tables and asked me to fill out some information. Soon, another producer (there were many) came over and asked me where my husband was. I told her he could not be there due to a business trip to Chicago. She then replied that the Executive producer, who was videoing another family, would not be able to meet with us since my husband was not there. My heart fell. The kids and I sat silently, watching the other family audition. The kids and mom were break dancing and laughing. Dad kind of sat in the background. David, our second son, turned to me and said, "Mom. Let's go home. We don't have a chance." I replied," We did not come all this way to turn around and leave. I'm not going until they tell us to." At the time, our oldest Jon was 15, David was 12, Chris was 10, Jeremy was eight and Michael was four. It was rather difficult keeping them quiet while I finished the paperwork. As I was wrapping it up, one of the producers walked over and noticed Michael sitting on top of a table. Mr. Michael has the longest eyelashes God could have ever given a boy. He also has chocolate brown eyes and hair. She scooped him up and took him over to the Executive producer. "Have you ever seen anyone so cute?" Michael proceeded to tell them that he played soccer, football, baseball and any other sport he could think of. Before we knew it, we were being interviewed without Dad. As we sat in front of a camera, the producer asked us questions about how busy we were. The kids rattled off all the sports they participated in, as well as the music programs they did in school. I shared how I had a music degree and had been in the music ministry for many years prior to moving to Houston. "The Beadles are quite a musical family. I would like a 10-minute video of your home. Anything musical you can perform, please do. And by the way, make sure dad is there. We want him to tell us how busy you all are." Our jaws dropped. We had made it through the first audition. On our way home, I told our oldest, "Jon, print off a Beatles song for us to perform." David hooked up his little electric drum set (easier on sound in an apartment), Jon played his electric guitar and the rest of us, including Dad, sang the Beatles' hit, "Help, I Need Somebody." Leo then proceeded to tell how busy we were. One week later, the executive producer was at our door with his camera wanting to interview Leo. I fixed him gumbo and the rest was history....We were psychologically analyzed, had security back ground checks done and we had to write down hour by hour, what each of us did on a weekly basis. The funny thing was that they never called Leo for information. It was always me. I would go to work, come home, and work until midnight preparing the requested information to be sent the next day.

Filming began approximately 3 months after our audition. Within a few days, our apartment was lit up like a Christmas tree. Whatever light we lacked, they purchased. All of a sudden, we had lamps and light fixtures everywhere. Even the beds had small white lights outlining each bed. The dining room had a Japanese ball hanging from the ceiling. They had sprayed it with tea.

Yes, tea. They told me it creates a soft or more dimly lit light atmosphere for a more intimate room. Each bedroom had one as well. The night before filming, the producers held a meeting with us. They told us we would be competing with a family of five girls. We were also given the rules of the game. There were four areas of competition: housekeeping, time management, parenting and nutrition. I was ok with time management and parenting, but housekeeping and nutrition made me a little nervous. After everyone left, we gathered in a circle and each person prayed a simple prayer. David said, "Lord, play and win this game through us."

Six am the next morning, there was a knock at the door. Filming had begun.

The boys were followed to school by cameramen, except for Jon who took a bus. Microphones were attached to the back of our pants. The actual microphone is attached to a wire that ran up through the shirt and attached to the inside collar. As everyone began to leave for school and work, I realized I would be the one being filmed most of the day. I was able to take off work since I was in the middle of changing jobs. They filmed me doing everything from folding clothes to cooking dinner -- you get the picture! They loved following me to the grocery store. Every time someone talked to me, one of the producers would run up to that person and have them sign a release form allowing them to be filmed. I could not have been happier than when everyone began to arrive home. We had to be at the baseball park by 5:30pm. It was full of rambunctious kids practicing or playing their games. Faintly, I began to hear giggling and chanting from the other side of the field. We noticed a large group of cheerleaders, doing flips and cheering, "BEADLES, BEADLES, WE WANT YOU!" We all stopped what we were doing, and quizzically walked over to them. As they continued to cheer us on for the show, we were presented with a photo album of our competition. There were pictures of five lovely girls and their parents, the Clarksons. It hit us like a ton of bricks: there was another family out there who had gone through the same process we had and wanted to win as much as we did. I told Leo, "If these professional cheerleaders are any indication of the surprises that await us, we are in for the ride of our lives." If they only knew where we'd come from...

Leo and I met at LSU in the summer of 1984. I was getting my Music degree and he his Computer Science. Everyday, we met with other friends for lunch. It was a safe place for cultivating friendship. While getting to know one another, we shared the same faith and desire to do God's will. One night I had a dream. I saw two people at the altar getting married. The bride was me, but the groom was definitely not the gentleman I was currently dating. It was my buddy Leo. I tossed the dream aside thinking it was surely the pizza I had eaten late that night. The Spring Semester finally began; Leo's roommates informed him they had found the girl for him. As they told him my name, his face lit with excitement, and they knew they had the right gal.

Leo had not dated in five years. He felt like he would know the right one when he met her. He did not ask me out right away. His roommates were busily telling me how much he liked me, but I wasn't receiving any phone calls from him. Valentines Day was fast approaching. "Lord, if Leo doesn't give me anything this Valentines, I'm writing him off." There, I said it. That blissful day, while eating in the school cafeteria, Leo presented me with a BIG Valentines card. I anxiously opened it to find a beautiful scripture. It came from the Book of Ruth. "And he said, Blessed *be* thou of the LORD, my daughter: *for* thou hast shewed more kindness in the latter end than at the beginning, inasmuch as thou followedst not young men, whether poor or rich."

"And now, my daughter, fear not; I will do to thee all that thou requirest: for all the city of my people doth know that thou art a virtuous woman." (Ruth 3:10-11 KJV)

He wrote, "Dear Ree, you are truly a woman of excellence. Sincerely, Leo."

I jumped up and gave him a BIG hug. Leo had not dated in five years. I caught him off guard by my obvious enthusiasm. He sheepishly grinned and quickly exited the cafeteria. One week later, he said, "We need to talk." I agreed and we walked over to a nearby park. At this point, he did not beat around the bush. "I have loved you since we first met last summer. If you don't love me, let me know now because I don't want our friendship to be hurt in any way." (I am nervously pulling the grass out of the ground), as I tell him, "I love you too." We hugged and went to class. Deep in my heart, I knew God was giving me a special treasure and his name was Leo Beadle.

Life was moving at a fast pace for this young 20 year old. I nervously laughed one evening and said, "Yeah, I'll believe I'm the one when you put a ring on my finger!" We laughed and he replied, "Give me a few days." I was not very anxious to get married. Yet I hated always wondering if this guy or that guy was 'the one' for me. At the wise old age of 19, I made a list of what I wanted in a husband. One being, that he would have dark brown or black hair (I thought brunettes were to die for!). I also wrote that he would love God more than me. That he would want children and be a good provider. And by the way, I did not want to marry a preacher. Okay, I hoped he would be rich and I could just be a diva and get my nails done, but truthfully, I wanted us to work together for our dreams and goals. I began to see how Leo met the criteria I had for a husband. I was also amazed by his generosity and kindness. He was a gentleman in every way. The only problem was that I was just coming out of a previous relationship. My parents were not very excited about the prospect of a new beau. I was, however, simply because I'm all about adventure and romance. Even at my young age, I knew the peace I had about Leo was different. I felt God's Mighty hand on our lives, even though it was happening so fast, I hardly had time to think.

March of 1985, my parents and I left for my cousin's wedding in Georgia. My family lived in New Orleans.

Leo agreed to pick me up at my house and drive me back to school. All weekend, even though I had a great time singing in her wedding, I was nervous about my new relationship. The drive back to New Orleans was uneventful. Suddenly, without warning, a quiet voice deep within me said, "You are getting married in December." Just like that. No thunder, no lightening bolts. It was a still small voice blanketed with kindness. That evening, Leo came to pick me up. He seemed very anxious while visiting with my family. Quickly, I decided to leave for school without causing him any more jitters. That night, while sitting on a bench in a nearby park, Leo Beadle asked me to marry him. I gave such a resounding YES! that I completely caught him off guard. "Are you sure? I know we are moving at a fast pace, but answer me again." I again replied, "Yes." He said, "Great because I have a ring and I think we should get married in December." I remembered that voice....We hugged and went to his apartment to tell his roommates the good news and to call my parents, whom we had just seen several hours before. The phone rang and my dad groggily picked up. "Hello. Leo Beadle? Oh. Hi. Thanks again for taking our daughter back to school. What? You asked her to marry you?" as he jolted out of bed. "Wait, here's her mother, talk to her." As usual, Daddy would hand Mom the phone when he was too overwhelmed to handle a sudden situation. Mom told Leo it would be best if he and I came the next weekend to discuss this news with her Dad. Leo heartily agreed, hung up and planned our upcoming visit.

Our few dates, and there were few prior to engagement, consisted of roller skating and eating out at restaurants that stayed open all night. One evening, in particular, we talked about the vision we had for our lives. Leo was concerned that because I was in music, that I would want to marry a preacher. Especially since my dad was one. Yes, I am a PK, or preacher's kid. I have two older brothers as well. Leo was very relieved to find out I did not want to be a preacher's wife. He told me he loved the computer field and wanted to pursue business.

I loved my parents and always honored them for fulfilling their callings, but that wasn't mine and I was glad to find out Leo felt the same way. My parents were totally caught off guard. They had only met him several times, the night he proposed, being the second. They invited Leo to spend the weekend at our home and tell them why he was asking for my hand so soon in the relationship. Dinner was set, and Leo began to talk. He told them he had not dated in five years. (He was 23 at the time.) "When I became a Christian, I asked God to show me when the right person came along," he told my dad with much confidence. Daddy leaned back in his chair and said, "Will you pay for her tuition and make sure she finishes college?" Leo gave a resounding YES SIR and the wedding plans began. Leo's parents, on the other hand, knew about our relationship from day one. He and his younger brother were the only ones not married in a family of six kids. They were ecstatic. His mom was even responsible for my engagement ring. (The first time we met, she ran to greet me with open arms and presented us with key chains that read, "I am my beloveds and my beloved's is mine." It was a day full of surprises, to say the least! The minute Leo took me home to meet the Beadles; it was love at first sight for all of us. We were the talk of the church and anybody else in town who cared to listen.

Our entire courtship lasted one month and the engagement lasted nine. We soon realized how different our families were in many ways. My dad was a Presbyterian minister, serving a church in New Orleans. Leo's dad was an Electrician, working two jobs. My dad was a violinist and Leo's dad wired homes and buildings. I was raised near St. Charles Ave in New Orleans and Leo was raised in Morgan City, Louisiana. Debutante parties and Mardi Gras were regular events for me growing up. Football games and crawfish boils were regular events in Morgan City.

Not that I was a 'deb' or anything, I was just a 'preacher's kid' who happened to live amongst those that were. I attended an all girl's Catholic school where I wore a uniform and PE was referred to as Sports class. Leo, on the other hand, attended public schools and worked with his dad from the time he was about 9 years old. Mr. Beadle found that his young son could fit in places he couldn't, so he was a great help when wiring homes. All of Leo's siblings were married with children except him and his younger brother. The only thing I had to worry about while growing up, was when the next audition for the school play was to be held. Leo grew up wondering when he could leave Morgan City and go away to college. He loved books and graduated top ten in his class. I graduated from High School and that was good enough! One thing was the same; our families dearly loved us. That love would sustain us through good times and bad.

December 28, 1985 graciously arrived in the form of an incredible wedding day. It was held at our church in Baton Rouge, Louisiana. Leo was so nervous he couldn't eat. I'd forgotten my $250.00 going away suit and my mom was in charge of the wedding reception. Did it sound stressful? It was. The moment I stepped out onto the isle though, a peace fell over my heart. I was marrying the man of my dreams. He was the kindest, sweetest, giving person I had ever known. I knew we were in God's perfect will and there was no greater feeling. We had three pastors marry us. Our present pastor performed the ceremony, Leo's family's pastor offered encouragement and wisdom, and my dad served us communion. After the service, we headed to the reception hall, where a feast awaited us. Disney World was our honeymoon destination, and we intended to have as much fun as possible. Waving goodbye to family and friends, we embraced our new life as husband and wife. Leaving college, Leo's first job laid him off soon after graduating. Not having quite enough money for the honeymoon, we charged most of the expenses. Disney is not cheap. The thought never crossed our minds to choose a less expensive destination.

Leo worked for an insurance company while I continued at LSU. I changed my major 4 times, so graduating was going to take a little more time than anticipated. We had one car, so I dropped Leo off in the mornings and picked him up in the evenings. For the next 2 ½ years, we continued this schedule. Church was and still is a very important part of our lives. I was involved on the worship team and we led a home group bible study. The years were very hard financially. Tuition, rent, utilities and groceries were difficult for us. I was not from a large family. I was used to my own space -- okay, my own floor. My brothers were quite a bit older than I was, so they moved out long before I did. We lived in the church's house. It was approximately 4000 square feet. I enjoyed lots of space, to say the least. Leo, on the other hand, grew up in a large family under an entire house that spanned 1200 square feet. He was used to sharing; I was not. I ate anything; he did not. My family had been exposed to cuisine from all over the world. Members of our church would cook for us or take us out. New Orleans is known for its incredible food. From crab meat au gratin to oysters on the half shell, I loved it all. Leo's, diet consisted of rice, red meat and gravy, white beans and gravy, spaghetti, fried chicken and occasional steaks. I thought I would faint when he announced, "I no longer want rice and I hate vegetables except for string beans. Oh, and by the way honey, I only want white meat in chicken." My cooking options were definitely a far cry from home. My dad always came home at 5:00 sharp and ate at 5:30pm every night. It may have helped that we lived only three blocks from the church, but I thought Leo should follow the exact same schedule. I was shocked when he strolled in at 6:30 p.m. because he was raised with the rule that you work until the job is done. After a few nights of sleeping in separate rooms, we decided that love covers a multitude of differences!

Leo and I always wanted kids. I knew he would make a terrific father, because he was so good with his own nieces and nephews. We agreed 3 years was a good time to wait to have children. However, my idea of 3 years was that on the 3rd year, we would be holding our baby. His idea of waiting three years was waiting before trying for three years. One weekend we were visiting our friends Brian and Sonda Brewster. While Leo was still sleeping, she and I tiptoed to the bathroom and I took a pregnancy test. Pink meant it was positive. Brian, Sonda and I, proudly stood at the foot of the bed Leo was still sleeping. We tapped him on the foot and I excitedly said, "Honey, we are going to have a baby." You would have thought a big gust of wind had knocked him in the face. "That's nice, honey." "That's nice honey?" Did he just respond like I thought he did? We politely left the room so he could get up and face his future fatherhood alone. Brian invited him to come to work with him that day. All Leo could think about was the financial responsibilities that lay ahead. I was still finishing my last semester at LSU, which meant he was still paying tuition, and we were still struggling to pay our bills. Did I mention he had changed jobs? He now worked for a department store in their IT department. Sometimes, while waiting for him to finish work, I would go shopping because they informed us that since Leo was an employee, we got an extra 20% off all merchandise in the store. I thought that was too good to be true. If we needed clothes, we charged it. At Christmas time, I always reasoned that Leo's family was so large I had to charge their gifts. The excitement of our new baby over rode any financial difficulties. We were going to have a baby. That was all that mattered!

Jonathan Andrew Beadle was born September 6, 1988. He was the thrill of our lives. Along came David Leo Beadle May 30, 1991, Christopher Joseph Beadle April 6, 1993, and Jeremy Samuel Beadle March 8, 1995. The first three were planned. We had four boys in 6 ½ years. By the time the fourth was born, we lived in a small town called Kinder, LA on an acre of land. It was the perfect place to have a large family. Leo worked about an hour away and I volunteered at the church as a choir director/worship leader. I wore many hats and loved them all. There was one small problem. I was and still am not a country girl. We moved there in 1990. I comforted myself with the fact that Wal-Mart was two blocks away. Six months later, it became the first Wal-Mart ever to close its doors. This meant I would have to drive 45 minutes to the nearest store. Kinder had two grocery stores, lots of churches, a town hall, one elementary school, a middle school and a high school. There was one streetlight and every night, we could hear the trains rumbling in the distance. "Why did we move here?" I asked Leo time and time again. As the years moved on, I began to realize that this little town taught this city girl how to slow down! The problem was, I didn't learn very quickly. As soon as I could, I was throwing the kids in the van and high tailing it to the city of Lake Charles LA as much as I could. We visited the mall, McDonalds, Wal-Mart -- anywhere we could be entertained. I felt that since Leo had to go to work an hour away, I had every right to take the kids places so we could stay entertained. Not to mention church 3 times a week, cub scouts once a week and baseball during the spring. I tried to be the perfect mom. I pureed fresh vegetables and froze them in ice trays hoping they would not inherit their father's eating habits. Jon wore cloth diapers until diarrhea spilled all over the car seat. I cooked 30 days in advance so our meals were inexpensive. Of course, this did not deter our trips to the city where we ate out as much as possible!

"Honey! Where is Christopher?" "He's probably running around the ball park!" Leo replied. After several attempts, I resigned to the fact I may have left him home alone. Let me tell you about our Christopher, now better known as Chris. At the ripe old age of four, he drew his own bath water and fixed his own breakfast. Believe me, I tried to do it for him, but he insisted it was his lot in life to be as independent as possible. I sped home in the beloved suburban, wondering where he could possibly be. I wish I could say he was safely tucked away in his room patiently awaiting my arrival. That was too boring for Mr. Christopher. He was happily jumping on our neighbor's trampoline, who did not seem to be home and who lived across the lake from our house. "Mom, I was playing Nintendo in my room, when I heard the car pull out of the driveway. I figured you would eventually come back, but I decided to jump on Alex's trampoline instead of being bored at home." There was also the time we left him at the Chinese Restaurant. We returned to find him happily playing with a little Chinese toothpick umbrella and watching the brightly colored fish in the pond. Of course, there was the day at the ballpark when Leo forgot Jeremy. He wandered out of the park into a nearby neighborhood. Someone found him and thankfully called the police. They came right over. The problem was, my cell phone was turned off and Leo was not answering his phone to a number he didn't recognize. When he finally did, Jeremy had the police take him to church, because he told them that is where we probably were (I guess because we were there so often.) Running up to Jeremy, expecting the worse, Leo's eyes widened in disbelief as Jeremy exclaimed, "DAD! I got to ride in the coolest cop car! You gotta see it!" We sometimes forgot one or two at church. One night, we had finished a weekend conference and just gotten home. The phone rang. "Rena Beadle, this is your pastor. We are entertaining your 2-year-old (Jeremy) at the minister's dinner since you left him at church." He was truly enjoying this moment! Gasp... we found Jeremy seated next to the guest minister, heartily eating a big bowl of gumbo. And of course, four years later, there would be a very unexpected fifth son.

The cameras jolt me back to reality. Those toddler years are long gone, but today, we're taping a national television show for a major network. The ride of our lives is fixing to take us on an incredible journey. Where or how, we do not know...

Chapter 2

Self-Employed -- Yikes!

Freddy, our house producer, had an incredible eye for detail. We would be going about our day, when suddenly there would be an orange envelope on a nearby table. Leo would open it, calling the entire family together. At that moment, he would read it out loud sharing with the kids what the next challenge would be. The rules were always stated and there was never a question as to what we were supposed to do. The envelopes almost always involved the entire family, as well as the fact that the Clarksons had to complete the same challenges with the same rules. No one knew when the envelopes would appear. However, teamwork seemed to be the name of the game. The most difficult part was that they never knew how well they were doing. That day was reserved for the Grand Finale. NBC knew all the activities of our lives, presenting challenges that either went along with what they already were doing, or totally interrupted their schedules with unexpected events. Suddenly, I recalled some of Leo's several early career positions.

Leo began as a Programmer for an insurance company. He then worked in the IT department of a department store, later a bank, and then for an oil company as a Systems Analyst. He is known better as our beloved Computer Geek. He loves solving problems and can smell a computer virus a mile away. We are extremely opposite in personality and vocations. He loves lists and checks each task off as he completes it. I love PEOPLE and spending time with them. He loves computers and I love singing! Downsizing became the corporate buzzword. He soon realized he was doing the jobs of three people and getting the same raises as everyone else. Just like in the reality show, he was rarely, or never told how well he was doing. He worked an hour away and sometimes traveled a week at a time. The children were very young and we missed him.

"Leo, I work for an Indian tribe near your family. I've run into some issues, I need your expertise. Would you consider partnering with me in business?" This gentleman helped network new buildings for an Indian reservation. By this time, Leo was tired of "Corporate America." It was 1998 and he felt like he was stuck in a rut. We also had quite a lot of debt. Raising four kids on one income and living like we had two, was getting old. He definitely needed to make the same amount of money as he did at the oil company. We had put Jon, our oldest, in a Christian school even though money was tight. Leo's partner was generous and excitedly, we launched into the partnership. Even though I am not computer savvy in the least, I felt a part of this venture because we have always encouraged each other to go for our dreams. There was no overhead for this new business, because the office was in his partner's home. Leo already had a few customers of his own, and together, they became one team. They networked new buildings, fixed computers for small businesses, churches and schools. Just like the reality show, they paid attention to every detail of the customer they were serving. The funny thing was that every time I mentioned it to successful business owners, they would shake their head and say, "Partnerships rarely work. Be careful." We just tossed those words to the wind. Life seemed great and we were going for it. Unfortunately, they were right. We learned a big lesson; someone's business ethics can be totally different from ours. Alan K. Simpson said, "If you have integrity, nothing else matters. If you don't have integrity, nothing else matters." There were too many questions about situations of which we were not made aware. Trusting someone with our financial future was a big step. As we walked in this situation, the sense of partnership and team spirit began to fade away. Sadly, the partnership only lasted 5 months.

January 1999 Leo and I opened Lake Area Network Technologies. We had THREE customers and a lot of excitement. That 'Excitement' was about all we had. Our kitchen became Leo's office. Our corporation was formed and he started running. The problem was, where was he going? Three customers were not going to support our large family. "Honey, can we get a loan for start up capital?" "Nope," he said. I never asked again. We had rarely discussed finances in the past, so I refused the urge to discuss them now. Ignorance was bliss, or so I thought! Word of mouth was our only advertisement. Business owners would tell other business owners. A church needed him one day, a doctor's office another. Just like the reality show, Leo never knew what challenges would arise on a daily basis, and just like the show, some were more difficult than others. There were many times I wondered about the financial status, but the lights stayed on, so I figured all was well. We had some great customers. However, when Leo serviced their computers, they usually stayed sound.

You may ask if there was a business plan. The answer is no. All we had was our corporation papers and enthusiasm. Alan Lakein wrote, "Failing to plan is planning to fail." Leo and I did not have the discipline to plan our future, let alone our business. Our philosophy was to work hard -- period. I knew how to sing and raise kids. Leo knew how to fix computers. There were so many aspects to owning a business we did not know. First, we had no idea as to the taxes we would have to pay. For instance, it was almost a year into business when Leo discovered that he had to charge a customer sales tax IF he took their computer apart. Month after month, Calcasieu Parish sales tax and the Internal Revenue expected to be paid. We did not demand payment up front. Our customers had 60 to 90 days.

Two years later, I suppose due to fear of starvation, or feeling like an island, we added a partner to our business. Once again, our excitement soared. We purchased a small struggling computer business and opened a storefront. Things were looking up! The mayor came and we had an official Grand Opening. People piled into our new little office to congratulate us on our new location. The ribbon was cut and the newspaper did an article the following week. Our new partner was so thrilled at the prospect of leaving his present job, he did so, that very next week. Now we not only had overhead, but another family to feed (It was a good thing his wife had a full time job). The best part was that we no longer felt alone. The worst part was getting our customers to pay on time. After approximately 6 months, our friend went back to work. He had a lot of integrity, but we were not financially ready for a full-time partnership. By then, Leo needed some help. He hired a young college student who could work for a lot cheaper and handle more of the in-office computer clients. These were clients usually who had home computers. We always paid our employee before we paid ourselves. He did good work and allowed Leo to stay on the road servicing businesses.

Health insurance was the last thing on our minds. It was one bill that did not matter, or so we thought…. "Leo, I had a dream last night." Tammy shared with my husband in church one evening. "I saw you and Ree with a new baby." As she gave Leo the biggest smile she possibly could, he leaned over from the church's sound booth and declared, "STOP EATING PIZZA LATE AT NIGHT AND LEAVE ME ALONE!" Silence. Our little friend quietly left him to muse over her words. A few days later I was substituting at the kids' elementary school. A friend saw me in the cafeteria, and waved me over. "Ree, are you pregnant?" I shot her a face of complete disbelief and adamantly shook my head. "No" "Well, I think you are. At your age, having already had 4, make sure you get proper rest." "What? Girlfriend, there is no way I can be pregnant." I had been substituting as much as possible since our fourth son was finally old enough to go to school. It supplemented our oldest son's tuition at the Christian school and provided for a few extra needs. Leo needed my help financially and we were excited about the thought of having all four kiddoes in school at the same time. A week later, "HOOOONNNEEEYY," I cried. "Can you come to the bedroom?" I pulled out the pink colored pregnancy test. We were barely making ends meet as it was and now an unexpected, EXPENSIVE package was arriving in 9 months. We shook our heads in disbelief. "Mrs. Beadle, you will have to have another c-section. This will mean quite a bit of money up front to the hospital in order to cover the operation since you don't have insurance," Explained our O-B-G-Y-N.

Leo had to pay the doctor $500.00 a month. I never realized just how much insurance actually provided. Missing a few payments did not go well with the doctor, so the nurse phoned us, "Mrs. Beadle, the doctor feels you should go to the charity hospital." The what? The tears began to fall. I loved our doctor, but with no insurance, there were not any other options available to us. At the same time, I refused to take the boys out of Christian school. Driving 45 minutes each way plus the tuition, was only adding fuel to our fire. I wanted to keep working, but was placed on bed rest for the first month of my pregnancy. The bills were mounting and I was too afraid to think straight. A lady in our church told me about a clinic and the Medical Card. I had never had considered government help in my LIFE. Card in hand, I waddled into a walk-in clinic where a lot of young ladies waited their turn. I was already 7 months pregnant and in desperate need of a doctor and a hospital. As the weeks continued, the boys were able to receive free dental and medical care. We had to put aside our pride and hope this was extremely temporary. There had to be a better way. Leo's business was growing, but so were our BILLS. November 18, 1999, Michael James Beadle was born 6lbs 12 oz. A perfect little boy was born at such an imperfect time. We liquidated Leo's 401K in an effort to stay afloat. We already had a second mortgage on the house. Our note had gone from $500.00 per month to $ 990.00 per month. Our cash flow quickly vanished as we tried to pay off credit card debt, house payments AND private school tuition. I had such a difficult time letting go of that school. I know many people right now, are having to cut back. If we could do that part of our lives over again, I would have immediately removed them. Leo worked night and day, driving from business to business. Whether he had a partner or not, he stayed on the road, working many hours, hoping cash flow would increase.

Yours truly, was the SECRETARY. On top of head cook, bottle washer and now mother of FIVE boys, I answered the phones. One afternoon, I was checking messages. "Leo, this is so-and-so. Whoever your secretary is, GIVE THAT GAL A RAISE. She is awesome on the phone." That complement was like a cool glass of water on VERY parched ground. I knew a raise was not going to happen, but feeling appreciated went a very LONG way. I started noticing Leo was great at fixing computers, but hated to bill collect. The list was growing longer and longer each day. Many times, customers' computers would work so well after Leo fixed them, they would not pay us until they broke down again, *if* they broke down again. Mrs. SECRETARY became the new BILL COLLECTOR. "Hello. This is Rena Beadle from Lake Area Network Technologies. Your bill is 90 days (or less) overdue. When do you plan on paying? We APPRECIATE (I said it with as wide a grin as I could so they would FEEL my LOVE over the phone.) your business. I do not mind coming today and picking the check up. What? Your accountant is out today? Sigh. Please leave her a note and mail it as soon as possible. Thanks and have a GREAAAT DAY." Click. There was also the time I threatened (ever so sweetly) to SHUT a client's computers down if they did not pay ASAP. Leo wondered why he got a phone call from that office, claiming Ree could come right away and pick up the check after we had just discussed that morning, how much they owed him. Fancy that. (Wink)

"Honey, I met an ANGEL." Leo decided I was joining Rotary. Meeting people has always been one of my strengths. Fixing computers is Leo's. "I want you to meet other businesses in the area and let them know we exist." I gladly attended my first meeting. I sat next to the sweetest lady. We began talking. "I'm a CPA." "Really?" I said. "My husband tells me we don't need one because CPA's wouldn't understand the type of business we have. Kindly, she responded that actually she COULD help us and handed me her business card. I thanked her and happily went home. "Honey, I appreciate your desire for an Accountant, but first, we cannot afford one, and second, as I have said before, she would not understand our business." Isn't it funny how we can feel a certain way about something that leads to the very road we never wanted to go on? I shook my head, and quietly went back to fixing lunch. Maybe he was right. I was only a musician and mom who happened to have good people skills. I knew nothing about balancing budgets. Then there was the lien on our business account several times in a four-month period. I had never heard of that word meaning anything but SLIM. However, one day I had $1300.00 in our account and the next day we had $37.00. They always leave a little so we wouldn't have a big fat zero. Apparently, my "A CPA would never understand..." husband had not been paying all of his sales taxes on TIME. The lump in my throat began to move to the PIT of my stomach. Would we ever see the light at the end of the tunnel? I did not want to let go of our Christian school and Leo did not want to trust an outsider with our finances. Ignorance was definitely not bliss at this point.

I thought a struggling business and the arrival of an unexpected child was enough stress in our lives. "Sugar, one never knows when one is fixing to meet the Lord." My dad never talked like that. He had battled Prostate Cancer for about 7 years. Lately, it seemed nothing was helping. My parents were about to celebrate their 49th wedding anniversary. Leo and I had them over for dinner October 28th, 1999. I was huge and sure it was all baby weight. We filmed my parents as they told how they met, became engaged and moved into the ministry. They were hilarious, fussing over when and where certain events happened in their lives. As dinner was served, my dad prayed over the food and our upcoming fifth baby. I will treasure that film the rest of my life. Michael was born November 18th and Daddy died December 3rd. All he got to see was a computer print out of his fifth grandson. We didn't know how we were going to afford to shut the business down in order to make funeral arrangements and minister to a grieving mom. I decided that to avoid a potentially tone-deaf singer at daddy's funeral, I would sing. I stood up, 40 extra pounds SINCE giving birth and not feeling very strong, and belted out the first few lines of Sandi Patti's Bethlehem Morning. Suddenly, a strength not my own, filled me, as joy flooded my heart.

"And he said unto me, My grace is sufficient for thee: for my strength is made perfect in weakness...." (2Corinthians 12:9)

Through the months ahead the Lord was carrying me and would continue to do so. I knew I could not make it without Him. The weight of grief hung heavily on my shoulders. We loved our new baby, but grief is a visitor that takes time to leave. It comes to stay when you least expect it. The uncertainty of our future caused me to miss my dad even more. Tears would come and I would have to sit and weep until relief invaded my sorrow.

Nothing else could possibly go wrong, right? Another sorrow invaded our lives in the form of a church split! Relationships were broken and hearts and dreams were shattered for many. Many people left and hearts were broken. Just when we needed our church family, we no longer had one. We made the painful decision to seek another place of worship. Everything or everyone that mattered to us seemed to be stripped away. "Why is this happening, God?" I felt bare. "Where are you?"

"His great works are too marvelous to understand. He performs miracles without number. Yet when he comes near, I cannot see him. When he moves on, I do not see him go. If he sends death to snatch someone away, who can stop him?" Job 9: 10 – 12a NLT.

My family still needed me. The ones I still had around me needed to drink from my love and kindness. I desperately needed to feel my Heavenly Father's goodness and mercy. The first time we drove into the parking lot of our new church, the sign read, Victory Worship Center, the City of Refuge. The Lord gently spoke to my heart, "I will heal you here." We were about to meet some very special people with hearts big enough for all of us.

Have I been daydreaming? What did the producer just say? I forget, we're actually filming a television show here. "Boys, quit fighting over who gets to wear a microphone!" I shouted. Each day, just like those reality show challenges, our lives had many unexpected surprises!

Chapter 3

Shattered Dreams

"Remember H-O-N-E-Y, this show is YOUR idea!" Leo exclaimed. The preparation period was exhausting. All seven of us had to get physicals, take psychological evaluations and promptly mail them the results. My phone rang day and night, requesting more information. I silently wondered if all of this was worth the time we were investing. We had never been on TV, much less a show where we didn't know the outcome! I reminisced back to 2001 and the uncertainty of our business. Could LA Net Tech become a success? What was the end result of our labor? We had been in business now for 2 years. Things were not getting any better. We never knew how much we were going to make month to month. The customer base was growing, but the bills were also. We kept hoping that some how God would reach down and miraculously, over night, make everything better. Leo was working at an attorney's office for the secretary who handled a particular area of law that caused him to think, especially when the next morning, there was a knock at the door.

"Who could want to talk to us at 6:00am?" I asked Leo as we sleepily walked to the door. It was the sheriff. "Honey, what does he want?" "We'll see," Leo replied. He handed Leo some papers, turned around and left. I was so confused. Had we done something wrong? It wasn't even light outside yet. All of a sudden, Leo's arms were wrapped around me. "Sweetie, I need to share something with you. The credit card company is suing us for the balance we owe. I ALSO need to tell you that I have not paid the house note in 6 months." I felt like a ball slammed into my stomach. I began to shake. "Why didn't you tell me?" "I didn't want to hurt you." He replied. Leo has always taken care of me. I guess at this moment, to a fault. He always had a difficult time saying 'no'. During the first two years of our marriage, I decided we needed a new car. His car worked fine, but the air conditioner went out. I told him that if it needed work, then we needed a new car. He didn't want to deny me, so off we went to the car dealership. It was those thoughts that began to bombard my mind.

"Yesterday, I worked at a law office for their bankruptcy division," he continued. "I began asking questions about who and why people declare bankruptcy. The secretary informed me that everybody from the one who stays home and watches TV all day to the hard-working man or woman who has come across tough times. We will probably lose the house." I quietly looked around our home, the place we had shared so many great times. "Well, we WILL walk this out together." I said. Tearfully, we held each other for what seemed like an eternity. The children began to awaken, and life somehow had to continue on as usual. It felt so surreal, like a dream I was going to awaken from and go on as normal.

I wept as I called some of my closest friends. "I feel like we've failed. All we wanted was our own business. It was something we could build together," I told them. As quickly as the gasps were heard on the other end of the phone, their kind words of encouragement followed. Nothing seemed to shake the knot in my stomach. Exhaustion and chronic stomachaches were a part of my daily life. One afternoon, I could not get out of bed from a nap. If I could just sleep, maybe this bad dream would somehow disappear. The doorbell rang. I had not bothered to shower or put on make up that day. Anybody who knows me RARELY sees me without makeup, let alone shampooed and styled hair. I slowly walked to the door and recognized our friend Kyle Sonnier. I smiled weakly and opened the door. "Hi Ree." (Kyle has a strong, booming kind of voice. He had been in my Easter play for that very reason.) He had just returned from the rice fields where he farmed every morning before working at his family's grocery store. His boots were still muddy, as he handed me a half gallon of ice cream.

"Trisha told me about what you guys are going through." I hung my head and tried desperately not to cry. "I came here to give you Leo's favorite ice cream AND to let you know THIS bankruptcy WILL NOT destroy you." He gave me a quick hug, got in his truck and left.

As I shut the door, the strength of his voice reverberated in my soul. There is nothing more miraculous as when a friend courageously comes forward during a crisis and offers words of kindness and encouragement. At that moment, I had a glimpse of hope.

"Where did all the debt come from," I asked myself. There were no fancy boats in our driveway. Our cars were far from new. Our clothes were either given to us or bought from sales racks. I cooked more than we ate out. I began to realize that from the moment we said, "I do," we also said, "Let's charge." And I don't mean going forward. I mean credit card charges. "Honey, it was on sale. I couldn't pass it up." It was those little purchases that grew with the wonderful interest rates attached to those 'easy to use' credit cards. For instance, following our second child's birth, I DECIDED we needed a new bedroom set. Again, my sweet husband FINALLY agreed and off I went with two our two small boys and purchased a king size waterbed and two nightstands. (Sadly, early on, the bed gave both of us back aches.) Looking back, we only paid the minimum payment. Leo even consolidated our credit cards. They just never seemed to go away. The saddest part was that I couldn't tell what we had bought that could bring us to such financial ruin. We had NOTHING to show for it. Cashing in our 401K did not help because we did not put that money into raising our home's equity. Like fixing the roof or installing new floors. The second mortgage decreased the value of the house.

The phone rang off the hook. "Hello. I'm looking for Leo or Rena Beadle." The hairs on the back of my neck would stand up. "You have a credit card balance of $$$. When do you plan on paying this bill?" "Uh, um, clearing my throat, "well, you see, my husband isn't home at the moment. He is the one who handles our finances. (Sigh,)" "Ma'am, we have a problem. We have not received a payment in over 3 months. I will call back tomorrow." CLICK. I did tell her the truth. Leo did handle the finances. Could that possibly be one of our MANY problems? I loved the idea of owning our own business and following our dreams. However, I seemed to run or turn my head from the day-to-day operations of accounting issues and BUDGETS. The phone continued to ring every single day. We didn't have caller i.d., so fear would grip me every time I picked up the phone. It just became easier to not answer the phone at all. The answering machine became my closest friend. If I didn't talk to a bill collector, then I could keep my head in the clouds and somehow emotionally survive the next day.

"We have an appointment with our attorney tomorrow afternoon," said Leo. The lawyer, who was a long time customer of ours, suddenly became known as 'our attorney'. He continued, "We have to list all of our debts, as well as our assets. He will review our information and advise us on which type of bankruptcy we should pursue." I definitely could not ignore the reality of our situation. We called Leo's parents to tell them our news. His dad began to cry. "Son, when you all were very little, we went through bankruptcy. I hate for you to have to go through this." He couldn't finish speaking, so his mom spoke up. "Honey, they took everything we had, except a rocking chair so I could rock my babies." We all sat on the phone and wept. She said that in those days, after removing everything from your home, they would hang a sign on the front door that read 'BANKRUPT'. She tearfully shared that the men that were sent over to remove their belongings didn't have the heart to hang anything on their door. History was repeating itself. I couldn't believe it! His dad had been in a partnership that had gone sour. Do you think we could have learned from his mistakes? I guess not. They graciously gave us the $500.00 fee to file. I didn't want to tell my mom. She was still grieving my father's death and trying to make ends meet herself. We had to write down every piece of furniture, jewelry, and every vehicle we owned giving an approximate assessment of each. It was a tedious process.

The attorney studied our information closely. "Leo, I am not worried about your business. It just takes time to build. Unfortunately, you have too much debt and not enough income." He explained that Chapter 13 is a type or reorganization bankruptcy, where a plan is created for the debtor to pay off his debts over a 3 to 5 year period. Non exempt property, such as a home, property, is kept. This person typically has enough predictable income to afford their regular bills as well as debt payments agreed upon by the courts. Chapter 7 is for those with insufficient income to pay their bills and outstanding debts. Nonexempt assets such as property, homes, cars, boats, etc are liquidated immediately. "I feel you have no other option except Chapter 7." We sat stunned. "You will lose your home and they will probably take your suburban." I definitely was not counting on the thought of losing our largest vehicle! They could not take Leo's car because he needed it for his business. The next sentence did ease some of my pain. "From here on, do not talk to your creditors. They will be notified immediately and your phone should stop ringing." YES. I offered a silent prayer of THANKS and nervously nodded my head in agreement. "I will see you two in court sometime in May," three months away. We shook hands and left.

More decisions had to be made. First of all, where were we going to live? Leasers run credit reports. I had been substituting, but it still wasn't enough to buy diapers and fill up the refrigerator. Living in the country meant Leo had to drive miles everyday to call on his customers. I guess it was time to request the unthinkable – FOOD

STAMPS. I hated the thought. If we qualified for the medical card, SURELY we would qualify for food stamps. By now, if there was any pride in my heart, it was melting away with each step I took as towards the food stamp office. Wall to wall people, from babies to older adults lined the walls of the main lobby waiting for their name to be called. "BEADLE, please come here." I think I forgot to share that this was my THIRD visit. I attempted twice before, but lost my nerve. "Ma'am, all we can give you is $280.00 a month." I was a little disappointed, but I left with what looked like a credit card and the ability to spend $280.00 more than I had before. I hid it in my wallet and breathed a partial sigh of relief.

May 31st, 2001 Leo and I walked hand in hand to the courthouse. I had never been in one before. We were met immediately with security. As we emptied our pockets of keys and cell phones, Leo suddenly became very nervous. The actuality of our situation seemed to be slapping us in the face. We were fixing to let go of our home, the place we had shared so many memories: Birthday parties, family holidays, choir fellowships or hanging out with neighbors in the back yard. The judge took his place at a table facing the people in the courtroom. As I looked around, I realized there were quite a few there in the same boat we were. We took a breath of relief and waited for our name to be called. Just like the food stamp office, someone called our name. "Leo and Rena Beadle, please come forward." We took our places at the table facing the judge. Sitting next to us was our attorney. As the judge was assessing our information, he asked us questions about our home and cars. I was bracing myself for when he would announce we would have to give up our suburban, when our lawyer spoke up. "Judge, this is my COMPUTER guy I was telling you about." He then winked at him and smiled. The judge responded by clearing his throat and said, "OH, ok." (He coughed slightly.) "I don't see why you have to lose your suburban. Both cars will remain in your possession." The gavel went down and we gratefully rose to leave. Our cars would remain ours. YES! Or so we thought....

It was Father's Day and we were headed to Morgan City to see Leo's family. It was about a 3-hour road trip. I had led worship that morning in church, still basking in that

"peace that passes all understanding"
(Philippians 4:7b)

The kids always looked forward to their Aunt Julie and Uncle Mark's swimming pool in the summer. Louisiana summers are hot and humid. Swimming parties are usually accompanied by crab and crawfish boils. These wonderful nautical creatures are immersed in a big tub of boiling water, beautifully seasoned with Tony Chacheres, lemons, and anything else the cook feels is necessary. Long tables are covered with newspaper and plastic garbage bags. We sit down to peel and eat seafood all afternoon. Grandpa Beadle, lovingly referred by many as PAPA, knows his 5 foot 1 inch daughter-in-law (that would be me) will come RUNNING if crabs and or crawfish are going to be served. I couldn't wait to get there. "BAP-BAP-BAP" "What is that noise the car is making?" I asked Leo. It was LOUD. We pulled over to a gas station. After a look under the hood, Leo sadly announced, "It doesn't look good!" Leo's family sat down with us the next day, as he told me the engine was out and we did not have the money to replace it. It had only been TWO SHORT weeks since bankruptcy court. We were now left with only one car. Since Leo needed it for his business, I was now home with five children and NO WHEELS for the entire summer. Did I mention we had four in baseball? We piled into that little 4-door car everywhere we went. I felt like Ellie Mae Clampet on The Beverly Hillbillies. How would I survive five kids in the country with no transportation?

It was time to give up our home. I walked through all the rooms, remembering all the good times we'd had. As I sat on one of the boxes, I prayed, "Lord, I want to thank You for all the wonderful times we had. I thank You for each room and every person that filled it." My heart actually felt lighter. I found myself thanking God for five great sons and an awesome husband. I even thanked Him for our bankruptcy! I decided trusting God was a whole lot better than grieving our loss. Peace flooded my soul. At that moment, He became the Father I no longer had. It felt good.

Thankfully, a couple from our church graciously leased us their four-bedroom house WITHOUT running a credit report! The problem was it also was WAY out in the COUNTRY. There were no stores in walking distance. As a matter of fact, this house had at one time BEEN the town's grocery store. Obviously, it was not any longer. There was also, no garage or covered carport for the one little car we had left. The natural elements in Louisiana are not kind to objects left out in the sun. If it rained, well you might as well place a canoe in the back yard and take a ride. It flooded every chance it could. The ages of the children were 12, 9, 7, 5 and 1. Entertaining them during the summer with NO transportation was a challenge. Keeping my sanity was another. "HONEY" I called my husband. "Jeremy won't eat his lunch. WHAT do I do?" I cried. "TAKE A NAP and try to get him to eat later." My patience was wearing thin with each passing summer day!

Facing fear was one of my biggest challenges. I grew up in what the Presbyterian Church refers to as a 'manse,' a house the church owns. My Dad received a small salary, but did not have to pay the mortgage or utilities. It seemed wonderful on the outside; however, every time we needed or wanted to paint a room, we had to ASK a certain committee. If we needed a new roof, for instance, the plan had to be submitted. Basically, they had to vote on every issue and decide when and how the work would get done. Fortunately, many pastors now have the option of purchasing their own home. Somewhere deep inside my heart, a fear of never owning my own home continued to grow. It took me and Leo TEN years to purchase our first home and now we were losing it. Job said,

"... the thing which I greatly feared is come upon me." (Job 3:25)

Fear was now staring me in the face. Instead of shoving it aside, I had to deal with it if I was going to survive emotionally.

Those days were hard for sure. Life is funny, isn't it? The uncertainty of a new business was similar to the uncertainty of participating in a reality show. Good or bad, the out come would ultimately be in God's hands. Except today, we were preparing for the world to watch us do what we had learned to do best; be a family!

Chapter 4

Remaining a Family

"Michael, do you like girls?" "I hate girls." The cameras rolled as Leo met with each son individually, to discuss the opposite sex. At the brave OLD age of four, Michael Beadle was not interested in that topic for one second. It was David's turn. He was 12 at the time and sitting still for a fatherly talk about girls, with cameras in their faces, was definitely going to be a challenge. Looking back to those earlier years, one-on-one conversations were vital to remaining a strong family unit.

"Honey, get out of the closet." It was a Saturday evening and the family was in the living room watching TV. It was nice and dark in my little cave. "You will never get out of this mess" "You are a failure and always will be," the voices in my head screamed. "God has forgotten you." "No, Leo. I can't get out. Leave me alone," I cried. He gently opened the door, knelt down, and pulled me up to face him. "You cannot hide. Remember? We are in this together." "Why is it so hard?" I complained. When are things going to get better? "I don't know, but God does, and all I know is to trust him." Leo always worked hard to make our lives as easy as possible. I thought he could fix anything -- except this! I slowly walked into our little den and saw five incredible gifts sitting or laying on the floor. They were totally engrossed in their Saturday night movie. We had decided that one night a week was Family Movie Night. It was our time to hang out and just be together. I realized that by isolating myself, I was choosing to believe the voices in my head over my Heavenly Father's. Looking at our children, it dawned on me that spending time with them, communicating through laughter, fun and tears, would ultimately be one of the keys to our emotional healing.

Church attendance has never been an option for me, especially since my dad was the pastor. Growing up, we had to be very sick or dying to miss. As a young girl, I had no idea the full importance of what gathering together with other believers would mean along the way. As a married couple, church was never an option. The kids followed suit. "I don't feel like going' to church, mom and dad," was not allowed. I used to watch my parents minister to people from all walks of life. Dad preached, married and baptized his flock. Mom fed, prayed for people and sang in the choir. Up to this point, I had never really grasped how important the church would be during difficult times. My love for music came from singing in our church as a little girl. "What a friend we have in

Jesus. All our sins and grief to bear..." I would belt it out with all the strength I could muster at 6 years old. Leo gave his heart to Christ in college. He loved going to church simply because he knew and still knows how Jesus forgave him and gave him a new life.

Within the four walls of our church was a strong family of people united in God's love. We never felt like strangers because everyone was there to reach out and encourage each other. The teaching, music and different ministries were refreshing to our weary souls. It was there we found encouragement and the strength to face life's difficulties head on. Sunday was the time Leo and I could stand arm in arm and offer God a sacrifice of praise. We were able to get our minds off the day-to-day responsibilities and acknowledge God's omnipotent power over our lives, as we would once again remember His faithfulness and our ever-constant need for Him. One weekend, I attended a women's conference. I could no longer resist the urge to go to the front and kneel at the altar. As I closed my eyes, I had a strong impression of Leo and me paddling a canoe surrounded by an endless ocean. We were rowing with all of our might. "Ree, you and Leo are working so hard. However, I am the captain of this ship." The voice was ever so clear. Immediately that little canoe became an ocean liner. There were so many people I could no longer see us anymore; there was only one clearly I could see. It was Jesus. He was steering our ship, not us. At that moment, I surrendered my hopes and fears to God. I felt a flood of relief fill the deepest part of my soul.

"We are having auditions for our upcoming Children's play. Your son, David, has just the personality we are looking for in the main role. Would it be ok with you if we could audition him for the part?" Lori LaFleur, our Children's' pastor asked eagerly. We were very honored. It was wonderful to know that the church leadership saw the gifts and talents in our boys and wanted to use them in whatever capacity they could. The word family truly described our church. They were all about relationship. Our little David was 10 years old at the time. He was and continues to be, one big ball of energy. He and the boys were always filming themselves singing or pretending to be Superman. They rarely needed an audience to entertain. All they needed was a video camera and a wink from mom or dad. The children gladly became involved in several ministries. The youth ministry offered home bible studies for Jr. High and High School students. It was great for my two oldest sons because they went to their own age group's Sunday night bible study. We lived in such close quarters, that it was nice for them to be able to express themselves in separate settings. The children were involved in Children's Church and Youth Groups on Wednesday nights. They looked forward to hanging out with friends in a safe place. Jon and David were involved in their High School and Jr. High School band programs. Every spring, the four oldest boys played baseball. Jon was busily playing his trumpet in the band, when he asked us for a guitar. We felt it was very important there was a balance between church and other activities. It was important that they develop social skills that would help them in any setting. We wanted life to seem as normal as possible, so they were not always feeling the stress of our situation.

I guess because I have a Music degree, my gifts have always been used in church. I served the Praise and Worship team and Leo helped out in Children's ministry. We also held a bible study in our home every Sunday night. We had some great times meeting together and praying for each other. It was important that Leo and I serve others during this time. Giving out of our own needs helped us remember that life is not always about us. It is about serving Christ and those around us. Giving of ourselves while still in pain ultimately set the stage for the miraculous. My friend Melanie later told me, "I enjoyed the times we spent with you guys, because you didn't walk around looking sad all the time." Believe me, we felt that way many times, but we surrounded ourselves with people who encouraged us. I confided in several friends on a regular basis. There were only a few. Others could not have emotionally handled the severity of our situation. Jesus had disciples and we have those intimate few that have experienced life with us. However, THEY are the ones that ultimately shared in our victories.

We had to get creative when planning family activities. Birthday parties were given at home. We had friends over, balloons, cake and gifts. Games were held outside, such as obstacle courses or water gun fights. Water guns can be bought in many shapes and sizes. They are inexpensive and fun for many hours. Sometimes parties were held in the park. There was always a pool or play ground equipment to keep everyone entertained. There is a lot to be said for homemade birthday parties. Many times the parents would stay and fellowship while the celebration continued. We also had living room picnics. Louisiana weather did not always permit long hours in the hot, humid sun. Peanut butter and jelly sandwiches provoked discussions about life, God and each other. We ate meals together, praying before each one. The kids loved to draw. Leo was Band Booster President for Jon's band. I thought it was a lot of responsibility for him when he worked such long hours. It proved to have a positive impact on him and Jon's relationship. Leo got to accompany the band on a trip to Universal Studios because of the fundraising we had done. Even though there were a lot of other kids, it showed our son how much his dad wanted to be a part of his world. We never missed concerts or games unless another child was sick. Becoming a family doesn't happen during karate lessons, loud parties or school pep rallies. Those are well and good, but we found it was the quiet moments before they went to bed, or sitting under tents made of comforters, that relationships developed. We felt and still do, that our kids are a reflection of us. We knew that time spent now was vital for their future, as well as ours. They have taught me so much about enjoying life in the moment, and not worrying about the next hour or day. There was less anxiety and depression when we were together, sharing life as a team.

Ours prayers were carefully worded with our children. We were honest in telling them why we left Kinder and moved to another home. However, when praying, we thanked God for our new home and surroundings. We focused on keeping a thankful heart. Bedtime prayers were the best. We would lay down with them, talk about school, church or whatever they wanted, and then pray about those specific situations. Staying thankful was not easy, but extremely important to these little fellas who had endured a lot of change: new home, schools, church and friends, in a short amount of time. Crises usually demand a lot from the people involved. We saw God's provision many times after those thankful prayers.

One particular afternoon, Leo and I had been in a heated discussion over, you guessed it, money (or the lack thereof). He then left quickly for work. The kids came inside from playing and I needed a miracle. I gathered them in the living room and said, "Guys, we need to pray for Dad right now. Jon, help me." We prayed a blessing for each child, and then asked God to give dad wisdom for his business and our provision. "AMEN," they all responded. As I walked away, I suddenly felt compelled to ask Jon what he was thinking as he sat quietly on the couch. "I'm thinking about a song by Rebecca St. James." He sang, 'Don't worry about your life. If you hold it too close, you lose it. Don't worry about your life. So won't you let go before it's gone?'" The lyrics melted my heart. I knew God had spoken and though I did not know what was going to happen, I could not worry.

"Consider the lilies how they grow: they toil not, they spin not; and yet I say unto you, that Solomon in all his glory was not arrayed like one of these." (Luke 12:27)

There was a special bond between this mother and her son that day. I will never forget that moment as long as I live.

Our oldest, Jon, is now 20 years old. He remembers those days, vividly. " When you're 13 you relate to kids artificially, usually what shoes you're wearing or what girl you're into at the time. When you buy shoes that only cost 50 cents, you develop an attitude that says you don't care. I believe that resonated so much with my fellow classmates that I had something else to say, other than whom I was "dating" or what shoes/logos I was wearing. At the time, I also didn't care who was popular and I didn't care for cliques so I related to people more on a personal level and tried my best not to look down on other kids. I recognized early on how cruel kids can be and my desire to not be like them. There was a loner mentality I developed and that seemed to draw people to me because I was not trying to impress anyone.

I saw very quickly what the bankruptcy was doing to my father. My father is, at heart, an entrepreneur and had started his own business then. It wasn't easy for him to have five kids, a failing business he fronted, and a bankruptcy at his heels. I cared deeply for my father's sanity. I believe it is a big blow for a man when he cannot wholly provide for his family. I learned quickly not to ever ask for the candy bar at the grocery store. Even today I never ask my parents for money or very much of anything. Finance was always the concern; our family always seemed to stick together though. I don't think any of my younger brothers remembered the bankruptcy years as vividly as I do.

It made me have a mindset that family comes first no matter what. Even when we were financially at our lowest point, I never felt as though my father's business was before us. I remember my father buying us "Lunchables" from the grocery store, and then see my mom freak out at him because he had used our last food stamp points on the stupid junk food because we had asked him to get us some. My dad was my hero then. Seeing how my father continued to love my mother made me want to be just like him when I get married one day. As Abraham Lincoln once said, "The greatest thing a father can do for his children is to love their mother."

I have become somewhat thick skinned in the financial department. I do not believe in debt and see how the media has deceived kids into thinking debt is a good thing. I am also a strong believer in hope. Hope is something that can easily be grasped, but not easily carried. If I do carry it, however, I know I can not only survive, but also succeed. My advice to other kids walking through tough times is not to be afraid! Learn to wait for things. Learn to stand by your parents and do as they say. Be especially kind to your father."

Our son, David, is three years younger than Jon. He recalls, "I've always been a very optimistic, happy-go-lucky kid. Growing up, if I could stay outside all day, whittling sticks with my pocket knife, playing in the dirt with no shoes on, or swimming in my neighbors pond, I wouldn't have had a care in the world.

I wasn't aware of my family's financial difficulties when I was younger at all. In fact, I didn't notice until I found out that we were using food stamps. The food stamps did embarrass me a little. I never brought them up with my friends, and I even, most of the time, lied about whether or not we used them. I also started to notice our finances weren't up to par when I started to over-hear my mom venting to my dad about his customers not paying enough, or not even paying at all. She would say that he was too nice to them, by not demanding the money they owed.

Other than a little bit of embarrassment, the financial problems never really got me down. My parents have always treated us with more care than any child could ask for. They have always had open ears toward us, no matter what was going on in the finances, or what happened that day at work. Because of their love for my brothers, and me there was always a peace in our home, and we knew everything was ok. There was always food on the table, and we always had a comfortable bed to sleep in. My parents are very strong people, and they never lost their composure in front of us. I never knew how bad off we were until I became old enough to understand, because they never showed it."

If there are kids going through difficult times, I have to tell them this: it is never too late. Keep your dreams and pursue them as hard as you can. Do everything in your power to perfect your skills and your passions. Offer to do little things, like helping around the house as much as you can -- this will make your parents' day a little less stressful. Offer to work to help the financial situation if the need is present. Do not get down just because you may not have everything you want. Think of it this way; if you had all the money in the world, there would always be something else to cause struggles. Do not just pray to God to change the present. Take actions NOW to change your future. When God gives you lemons, don't just make lemonade, make the best lemonade you possibly can. When God gives you a passion, don't just accept it, chase after that passion as fast and as you possibly can." Children are so resilient! Looking back, it seems Leo and I felt the transitions of moving and changing schools much harder than they did. I was so worried they would be scarred emotionally. It seems it only made them stronger, more determined to keep dreaming. Our boys were and continue to be our inspiration.

"Leo, that was INCREDIBLE," our producer exclaimed. Leo had just finished his 'girl talk' with David, when the cameras shut down and the door opened. Freddy never let Leo know how he was doing in the show. However, he was overwhelmed by the level of communication between this father and his son. Those relationships didn't start during the show… they were nurtured years before when all we had was each other.

Chapter 5

Faith vs. Presumption!

I awoke with a knock on my door from the house producer. "Got to get up and get going. Busy day ahead" he said. So I shook the sleep off my eyes and shouted a wake up to the boys and jumped in the shower. A short thirty minutes later, we were all up and ready to go complete with our usual hidden microphones and tailed by cameras. On our kitchen table was another one of those "orange envelopes" they used to announce "chores" for us to do. We opened the envelope with some nervousness. I began to read how we were to face the other family in a one-on-one competition. The competition was to be mechanical bull riding! The boys and I were jazzed! We were to fly to San Antonio for the head-to-head contest. Our excitement was growing by the minute. We were going to show those girls what the Beadle boys were made of!

Having come to faith in God late in life, I often assume that I am somehow behind other believers who may have grown up in the church. So I try to over-compensate by jumping in headfirst when I learn something new about God. That is how it was when it came to "believing in faith" for God to somehow meet my needs and bless my family and me. It would take many years of struggle and an eventual painful journey through bankruptcy before I would mature in my faith.

Believe it and receive it! Name it and claim it! Speak it, see it, and receive it! These are statements I had heard at one time or another during my spiritual upbringing. Being a part of the "faith" movement, these concepts were central, or core, doctrines -- or so it seemed. Now I want to make it clear that I do not want to come against anyone who has said these statements. I have just come to realize that there is a whole lot more to our faith than a simple catch phrase.

As new believers we hear statements such as these and think, "Well that is simple enough, I'll give it a try," and off we go to conquer the world and see the wonderful hand of God move on our behalf and everyone marvel at our incredible spiritual insight. Then, when things fall apart as they often do we fault God and ourselves and sometimes even leave the faith we once held and cherished. I want to encourage you if this is you. God is way too big to be put into a box. He will not be your domesticated divinity. He is the sovereign creator of the universe. That includes you. So when things don't go as expected, ask Him to enlighten you and guide you.

Let me share with you some of my "leaps of faith" that turned out not so good early on in my Christian walk. Most of these came after Ree and I married. First, I had a good job working for an oil company in I.T. For those of you who don't know, "I.T." that stands for Information Technology, a fancy word for the computer department. I helped design, build, and maintain computer networks and services for the user community at a large refinery. Really was a good job with great benefits. Enjoyed working there and the people I worked with. One day, a co-worker asked if I could help with an outside customer he had that was having some problems for which my skills were particularly suited. I agreed and off into the world of "moon-lighting" I went. After a time of doing this, this same co-worker needed help on a larger project. I agreed to help and we had some success in it. He then convinced me to get the same certification he had. He then said, "If we can't make it out there now, nobody can." My pride wouldn't let that go, so we set a date to embark on our great self-employed adventure. I quit my job with little more than a hope and a dream of making it "big" on my own. We had no capital, very few clients, and a lot of debt. Not very smart, I would say now. I would advise myself not to do something so foolhardy; but then at this point, I wasn't really seeking or taking much counsel. Six months later my partnership was dissolved with my co-worker. The business folks will tell you that the form of business that fails the most is partnerships. I can see why. We thought we were so on the same page at the first. Six months later we discovered we had some irreconcilable differences in philosophy. So here I was six months after leaving my job with no income, a mortgage, and a wife and four kids to support. I should have picked up the phone, called my old boss, and asked for my old job back. Did I do that? No. My pride would not let that happen, so we kept plugging away at it. Building the client base one customer at a time. My customers liked me. The business was growing. It was not fast enough, however, to support us. We were using credit in completely unwise ways to keep us afloat until it all came crashing down.

Now in the midst of this I want to share another even more stupid decision we made in "faith." We know God wanted our children, which He had given us, to be educated in the most excellent way possible, so we sent them to a private Christian school. These are not cheap. We were spending over eight hundred dollars a month to keep our kids in this school. It was a wonderful school to be sure. But should you be spending money like that when you cannot even pay your mortgage? Of course not. This is where we would play our faith "trump" card and say, "God will provide."

Now certainly I believe God is our provider. However, He is not our magic vending machine. He sets specific conditions on whom and what He blesses and what He does not. For one thing, we cannot PRESUME on the blessing and provision of God. This presumption of God's provision is where I and I believe most Christians that are raised in the faith movement get it wrong. Presumption is not faith. What do I mean by that? Well, it is difficult to explain in words. If I described the two in words, they would sound the same. What separates them is not in the thought process or the attitude of expectancy but in the unlikely place of relationship. We presume on the blessings of God when we know enough about God to know that His desire is for our good and then we run off and act on this notion. We have faith that God will provide when we know about God's nature and desire toward us AND we have spent time with Him in our prayer closet in fellowship and communion with Him. It is one thing to know about someone. It is an entirely different thing to actually know someone. The same holds true with the Lord. Above all else, He not only wants to know us, but He also wants to be known by us as well.

One of my favorite ministers is Graham Cooke. He is a prophetic minister from England. I have never met him in person, but have listened to several of his teaching tapes. In fact, I have listened over and over again. If you spend much time with me, sooner or later I'm going to quote him. For me, he has just helped put a real clarity into my walk with God. Graham likes to say, "God is the kindest person I've ever met in my entire life." Wow. Just let that sink in for a few moments. Is that your perception of God? Having gone through the difficulties we've seen, I would certainly have a hard time with that statement.

However, even through the hard times, He never left us, or forsook us. It is through Graham's teachings that I have learned God is not the least bit interested in our comfort. He is, however, keenly interested in our growth and development and maturity. Moreover, God wastes nothing. We make stupid decisions and call them steps of faith. Then we end up in some terrible mess of our own making. Then the Lord in His mercy guides us up and out of it and through it all teaches us to be wise and think more like Him.

What I am trying to say to you is that you cannot have faith in someone you do not know first hand. You only trust someone if you have history with them. Trust is just another way of saying you have faith. You have faith in your employer to pay you every payday. Why? Well, they have proven trustworthiness by doing it repeatedly. That is a form of relationship. We have faith in God because we have history with Him. We have spent time in prayer and fellowship with Him and His spirit so that we have seen Him fulfill His words to us many times. We have seen Him fulfill his spoken or some would call Rhema words to us as well as His written or Logos words. As you read the Bible then His spirit will reveal and speak to you through it. Then you see the Word work in your life. You can trust it. You have a history with it and a relationship. Because you have seen Him come through many times before, you have the reason to have faith in what you do not see. To paraphrase a dear and departed great Christian named Francis Shaefer, "There are good and sufficient reasons why I believe what I believe. It is not blind faith."

When I say that faith is not stupidity, I am talking about presuming that God will do what you want Him to do. I'm sorry. Maybe that works for you, but I doubt it. In my experience, I have found that God does what He wants to do. The only time that benefits me is when I align my "want to" with His "want to." After all, shouldn't we all be dead as the scripture says,

"I am crucified with Christ: nevertheless I live; yet not I, but Christ lives in me: and the life which I now live in the flesh I live by the faith of the Son of God, who loved me, and gave himself for me" (Galatians 2:20)

So when we placed our children in an expensive private although Christian school and contracted to pay the tuition we were "presuming" that God would provide. We were not in faith. We just presumed that because God loves us and is good and wanted our children educated in the best way that He would supernaturally provide. God is not obligated to pay any debts he did not incur. On the cross, Jesus paid the debt He did not owe. He only funds the projects he authorizes. He did not authorize my kids' education at that private school. He wanted me to pay attention to Him in the secret place of my prayer closet and find out what He really wanted me to do. But I was too busy – that is, really worried – to stop and ask. I knew His will; or so I thought. Really, I just knew the testimonies of other saints that God had provided miraculously for in so many ways. I presumed He would do he same for me. After all,

"God is no respecter of persons," (Romans 2:11)

Right? Wasn't I standing on solid scriptural ground? Yes, and no. Sure God makes these promises. He is not a respecter of persons. What he did for one, he will do for another. He is, of all things, just, and justice demands He keep his word. He does keep his word -- His whole word. The problem is that I tended to "cherry pick" the parts I wanted to work for me. That is not how it works. You have to obey and operate in the whole of the word. Line upon line, verse upon verse; here a little, there a little, until you glean the whole counsel of God. There is safety in God's counsel.

"His word is a lamp unto my feet and a light unto my path." Psalms 119:105

What I wasn't doing is letting the entire Word light my path. I just meditated on the parts I needed. This is the recipe of how to move away from faith into presumption and headache and heartache and pain. I know what I'm writing here is not the popular mantra of the faith movement. However, I have learned that having faith is not just reading one promise out of God's Word, closing the book and then proceeding headlong as fast as you can with your ideas of what it means. After the meltdown and subsequent bankruptcy, we emerged as very humble people. God brought several mature older men and women into our lives. They helped us heal and begin to think through all of the dumb things we had done and move past the mistakes of our past. I thank God for His endless mercy and grace to us during this time. Two of these men continually challenged my thinking. I didn't like it at first, but today I love it when someone challenges my thinking. I have discovered that my thinking is not very good unless it is enlightened and inspired by God's thinking and His Word. Then my thinking becomes His thinking. Then my words reflect His and they have power and effectiveness.

Enough waxing spiritual! I'm of a melancholy temperament. If you do not know what that means then just suffice it to say I like order and predictability. I tend to be practical. So practically speaking, what can I offer you, the reader, to help you avoid these things in your life? Well, for one, listen to other mature and experienced believers. Seek the wisdom and counsel of others who have gone before, people who hear God's voice and know His ways. Remember as you seek counsel that you should always consider the source. For example, do not take financial advice from your broke uncle Earl. Use some common sense. By the same token, if you are getting great financial advice from a successful person whose marriage is on the rocks then don't take marriage advice from him. Find someone else who is successful in that area. I don't take advice from people on how to make a million dollars unless they are millionaires. I don't take marital advice from people who have been divorced twice and are in the middle of a third. I know this sounds simple, but it is amazing how many of us just ignore this simple principle and take advice from the wrong sources. Seek out successful Christians in all areas of life and glean truth and guidance from them. It will save you years of pain.

Do not expect your journey to be pain and trouble free. Even if you take our advice and do your best to avoid the pitfalls we had you will find your own. That is just life. Do not blame anyone for your trouble. Take responsibility for your actions and mistakes and learn from them. Get up, dust yourself off, and get going again. Life is too short to stay down wallowing in the muck and mud of your failure. Always remember that ALL success is built upon failure. Pause and think about this for a minute. Every time you ever learned anything in school or on the playground you first learn how not to do it before you learn how to do it right. Your coaches and teachers kept working with you until you got that swing right, or that serve right, etc., etc. Life is no different. We are going to make mistakes. Just be sure you learn from yours and others and develop the skill of success.

"God is our refuge and strength, a very present help in trouble." (Psalm 46:1)

He will bring the right people and opportunities into your path IF you allow him to!

On the subject of marriage let me go into one problem I had and had it bad. I kept financial matters to myself and did not share with Ree. I know her personality did not want to be bothered with it anyway. That should not have kept me from bringing her in to the process. It was a terrible error. Had I brought her into more of the family's financial matters, I could have avoided many things. By the time the Sheriff served us papers from the credit card company, I had not paid our mortgage in several months. My wife had no idea. Sounds pretty dumb, I know. It was dumb. Ignoring problems does not make them go away. In fact, they tend to get bigger left alone. I've learned to face them head on immediately. Deal with them now! Ree had been on me for years to develop a budget to order our finances. I resisted because I knew that it would not work. As Dave Ramsey says, "I was different." Not really, I was just stupid. I knew there was more money going out than was coming in and I knew I could not balance a budget. So why did I just keep going in that stupid dead-end route? Cause I had faith! Yep, God was going to bail me out supernaturally. Well, He didn't. And since our bankruptcy, we have lived quite successfully on a budget. It is a simple tool that can bring such peace into your life. Yes, it is limiting, but then, so is your income. That is why it works. You don't spend money you don't have. It is so powerful that it escapes "smart" people like me (Ha ha).

During this time, I read a book on finances that explained the way to get out of debt. Step 1 was to stop going into debt. Stop spending more than you make. That simple step I refused to take. I thought I had no choice in the matter. I had a choice. You have a choice. No, you may not be able to keep your toys, but you can stop going into debt. I could have pulled my kids out of that school. We eventually had to anyway. So, the bottom line financially is this: get on a budget. Make sure your spouse and you are on the same page with the budget or it will not work. It is basically an agreement or contract between you two that this is how we are going to spend the limited resources we have. Set your priorities together and stick to them. I am not going to tell you how to spend your money, but God's Word does set down some basic guidelines. You should first give to the church. Some call it tithing. I am not going to argue the 10% of net/gross etc. just make giving to the Lord your first priority and the rest will fall in line. Second, you should pay yourself first. This means start/build savings -- an emergency fund if you will. After that, create a budget for your living expenses including your mortgage, insurance, food, clothing, etc. Then save some at the end to enjoy. Everyone needs some "fun" money otherwise, life and this budget will be seen as an enemy. If you do the work and work the budget, it can free you of debt and give you "options" as Dave Ramsey says. For more on getting out of debt pick up Dave Ramsey's book "The Total Money Makeover." This book has helped us beyond measure.

So what about San Antonio? Well, we flew to San Antonio and met the other family at a western dance hall that had a mechanical bull. Then we waited for hours for the lighting guys to get the light "just right" for the shooting of that part of the show. The producers then came to us with the worst news that could have been given to me or my guys. The higher ups at the network had nixed the bull riding competition because it was too dangerous. Instead, we were going to have an eating competition with unusual foods and such. To say that this took the wind out of our sails would be an extreme understatement. I'm a very picky eater. Most of my boys are as well. In fact, I have often said to my wife and friends that I'd love to go on the "Fear Factor" show except that I would not be able to even begin the gross eating part. Here I had to do just that. I prayed and asked the Lord for grace and put a happy face on. I tried to encourage the boys as much as I could but was not very hopeful. Sure enough, we got creamed in the competition. I choked and gagged back as much of an incredibly gross sandwich made by the other side as I could before calling it quits.

After this, we headed back to the airport for the return to Houston. We had to wait over four hours for our flight because we missed the initial reservation. I felt betrayed. I felt cheated. I was angry. I just wanted to cry. What started out that day as an incredible high went to an incredible low. I was emotionally wrung out. I had feelings of extreme anger and disappointment welling up inside of me. I wanted to go over to that producer and give him a piece of my mind and tell him just how unfair it was to mislead us and on and on. But in the midst of this incredibly painful situation, I felt the sweet hand of God speaking through my pain and telling me not to act on my feelings. I excused myself from my boys and went to the bathroom where I got on my knees and asked God to help me not to dishonor Him. I wanted to glorify Him. I made several trips to the bathroom over the next couple of hours. My emotions did not just magically come under control. I was in the battle of agony for hours. I cannot begin to express how difficult it was. Maybe I can understand at least in some very small part what Jesus went through in the Garden of Gethsemane, but probably not. At any rate, I managed to keep a good attitude and get home that night and into bed without making any big deal of what happened. That in itself was a victory. It would not be until the final outcome of the show that I would fully understand what God was doing. Just as I felt trapped during the food competition, I felt trapped in my business. However, like the show, God's grace and peace enabled me to make it through without allowing anger and frustration to get the best of me.

Chapter 6

Get Up!

"Sir, I am a Private Investigator with NBC. We run criminal reports on contestants for reality shows. Your name was submitted by Leo and Rena Beadle as character references on their behalf." Jody LaFleur was the Worship pastor for our church in Sulphur, Louisiana. He told them that we now lived in Houston and attended Lakewood Church. "Lakewood Church? My husband and I love watching Joel Osteen on TV. As a matter of fact, we are Christians." Filming had already begun, but I could not help but remember Pastor Jody relating that phone call to us. I sensed God was up to something bigger than us just getting to be on TV. It had only been a few years earlier that all I wanted to do was give up. I felt like an airplane on autopilot; I was simply going through the motions of life. There were times when putting one foot in front of the other required a lot of will power. It was difficult for me to help Leo in his business because all I wanted to do was run. He took on the full responsibility of answering all of his calls, visiting customers, and keeping the books. I, the one who had encouraged him to go into his own business, could no longer help him. Our stay in the 'grocery store' house was coming to a close. We found a little rent house closer into town near Wal-Mart. There was only one bathroom and three bedrooms, but we were close to Wal-Mart. There was a wonderful park at the end of the street that had a community pool and library. Another move meant more packing and unpacking. It seemed like the story of our lives. If Leo didn't work, we didn't get paid, so most of the preparation would be on my shoulders. Our home bible studies were still happening, but not much was happening. We had small numbers in attendance. I would lead worship, but not feel anything. I'd belt out Israel Houghton's song, "You are good, all the time. All the time, You are good," all the while thinking, "How are we going to make ends meet this week?" or "I sure hope he is good, all the time." It seemed that nothing we did prospered. Once again, the closet looked awfully inviting.

"Ministry organization is changing. Gary and Pam Babineaux will now be over you and several other home groups. They will be visiting your bible study very soon." Our pastor had called to give us the news. We were excited about the change, basically, because we were DESPERATE for someone to help us with our dwindling bible study. We were also apprehensive. We were still in our little grocery story home, fixing to pack up and move to another little home. Were we spinning our wheels? To add to our nervousness, the Babineauxs were an extremely successful couple in our church. They had it ALL: THRIVING businesses, children and grand children who all lived near them on their BEAUTIFUL ranch. We worked all Sunday afternoon preparing for their visit to our bible study; we vacuumed, dusted, washed windows and prepared dinner. Lately, we never knew who was going to show up. They arrived on time. We hugged and immediately invited them in. Gary is a giant on the inside even though he is not a big man on the outside. After scanning the house, he spoke. "You guys do not have to live like this." I felt that old ball hit my stomach again. "You are both some of the most talented people in our church." Well, that was a nice statement. I took a breath. "Ree, God says you talk too much." What? Ouch! Humiliation gripped my heart. "LEO," Good, it was his turn now. "IF you will submit to my authority, I will teach you how to succeed in your bible study, finances, every area of your life. However, if you do not submit, I will never speak to you about this again." Leo nervously nodded his head and promised to submit. Even though no one showed up that night, we had our bible study, ate, and they thankfully left. I turned to Leo and said, "WHO does that MAN think HE is, coming into a home I spent HOURS cleaning, telling me 'We don't have to live like this'? OBVIOUSLY, our house isn't GOOD enough." "Honey, that is not what Gary meant at all. I need help. We need help. Please do not be offended." I decided at least to try to understand. Shame and embarrassment can often masquerade as pride and self-preservation. This couple was fixing to change our lives in a very unexpected way.

"Ree, this is Pam Babineaux." Ugh. What did she want? "The Lord has instructed me to have a bible study on Friday afternoons for the wives of our home group leaders. It will last five weeks" Another Bible study? I was loading up boxes to move. We had to be out of the house in one week. I sat down on our couch. I did not have the strength for one more church-related activity. I wasn't even sure God was hearing my prayers anymore. As I drove past the gates to their ranch, the Holy Spirit gently said, "I want you to attend these meetings." "Fine," I replied. "I will, but I don't feel like it." Pam had us sit around her big dining room table. "I've been in prayer for each one of you. There are specific things He has shown me. Each week, I am going to teach you God's Word while cooking a special dinner for you. You all are responsible for bringing a scripture or song that has ministered to you throughout your week" I began to get very agitated. I had to bring what? "Listen people," I began, "I am tired. Unlike many of you, I have to be at church three times a week for the worship team. You have the choice to take a break if you or your family is extra tired. Right now, we continue to struggle and I am personally exhausted. Another thing..." I was feeling' rather in control and proud of it. "Pam, I have been disappointed in many a church leader. I will test everything that comes out of your mouth." I then took a breath and sat back. All the ladies seemed to sit there in shock. "Ree, I hope you do test everything I say. I want you to know something else about me. Gary always took excellent care of me financially. He set goals as early as High School, and met them very quickly. However, that early Sunday morning, as I knelt by my son, DEAD on those train tracks, all of Gary's money could not bring Josh back to life." I quickly sat up. "From then on, every breath I took had to come from the Almighty Himself. I learned some valuable lessons that, hopefully, you girls will allow me to share with you. You see, I like Martha in the Bible, was busy serving the Lord and my family. The traumatic death of our beloved son paralyzed me from the business of life. I chose to become like Mary and sit at Jesus' feet. Ree, you sing very well, but you sing NOTHING like when God's Presence is on you. You must SEEK HIM with all of your heart." My eyes fell. I quietly asked God to forgive my doubting and unforgiving heart. I knew these next 5 weeks were going to be a journey, one I was now willing to take.

The day arrived for us to move. There was a knock at the door. Several ladies from the bible study showed up with food and moving help. They helped us pack up one house and unpack the other. Instead of feeling overwhelmed by my circumstances, I was humbled by their selfless generosity. Receiving God's blessing was rather difficult. It's easier to help someone else in need than be the one who receives. We settled into our new little rent house quicker than I ever could have imagined. The love they showed me, gave me the courage to set aside time every morning to seek the face of God. The Friday afternoon bible study was different than any other because we all had to come with something we had learned from our quiet times with God. We weren't gathering to merely discuss life's hardships. We were learning to seek God for ourselves and bring something to Pam's table. It was something that would change each of us in our own special way. At first, rising at 5:30am felt like torture, especially after moving boxes and furniture. Soon, it became a pleasure. I looked forward to meeting with the Lord. She advised us to have communion during our quiet times. (Read 1Corinthians 11:24 for those who may feel a Pastor or Priest is the only one who can administer this sacrament, I strongly suggest then visiting your church several times a week during rough times to partake in Holy Communion.) I could see Jesus, preparing to die. He was letting his closest friends (and enemy) know of his imminent death through the shedding of His blood. It is amazing to me how he chose to fellowship with them around a dinner table, as He explained His sufferings. My soul felt clean, as I fellowshipped in His Presence. We are clothed in humility when nothing else matters, but Christ in us, our hope of Glory!

"Ree, share what you felt God showed you this week in your private time with Him." Why did Pam have to call on me first? "Psalm 91," I nervously replied. "Sing it." What did she just ask me to do? I sighed, opened my bible and began to sing that ancient song. Psalm is another word for song. King David wrote many of these 'psalms' as prayers to God. Some of them were songs of praise and thanks giving, some expressed his grief towards his enemies and many were written to express his love to God. I noticed David felt a lot like me.

"He who dwells in the secret place of the Almighty will find rest in the shadow of His wings. I will declare of the Lord, He alone is my refuge, my place of safety. He is my God and I am trusting in Him for he will rescue you from every trap and protect you from the fatal plague. He will shield you with his wings. He will shelter you with his feathers. His faithful promises are you armor and protection...." (Ps. 91:1-4)

David was anointed to be king long before he was actually crowned. His predecessor, King Saul was a jealous man and sought to kill David for many years. David would run and find shelter in caves, or SECRET places away from Saul. It was there he found shelter and protection until he could once again rise up and go forward. As I sang, strength filled not only my heart, but also the hearts of all the ladies there. From then on, Pam expected me to sing to them. I thought I had lost my song. Sadness and disappointment slowly began to disappear when I sang. Each morning, I went to my secret place and sang the psalms. I had sung for many years, but this was different. I sang from the deepest chamber of my heart and God began to speak.

She would go around the room, asking the ladies to share. Each one had a scripture or thought that would lift all of us from our places of despair. We would follow Pam to the kitchen. As she prepared our lunch, she would teach us. She compared natural food to spiritual food. The detail that goes into creating a wonderful meal is similar to our spiritual food. She went on to explain that God's Word is a detailed love letter to us. It is as vital to our spiritual nutrition as food is to our physical well-being. She took us on walks around her home. "Look at those plants outside. How does one differ from the other?" We replied that one was healthier and greener than the other. She said it was like us. When we walk with the Lord and trust Him, we are like strong green plants, properly nourished and able to withstand harsh natural elements. I knew I had been the wilting plant, so concerned about today.

"And he shall be like a tree planted by the rivers of water, that brings forth his fruit in his season; his leaf also shall not wither; and whatsoever he does shall prosper." (Psalm 1:3-7)

Pam helped us notice God's handiwork in order that we might desire to see His Greatness. During the studies, I realized I had gotten so caught up in telling God how awful I felt, that I had forgotten how much He loved me. I had to learn how to be quiet. That has never been my greatest gift. I began to quit dwelling on my situation and reached out to the other ladies. We prayed for each other and shared our goals and dreams. We became a mighty voice of praise as our hearts and minds were restored.

A journal was a great place for me to record what was changing in my heart and life. My prayers became bolder. I was crying less and thanking God more. I love journaling. I write teaching notes, special quotes from books, favorite scriptures or prayer requests. It became a type of therapy to spend quiet time with God and write whatever was on my mind at that time. I also closed my eyes and pictured myself sitting on a beach next to Jesus. I would write about those moments when I could visualize the waves rushing up to meet us. I knew the Living Water lived in my soul and He was refreshing me like no one else possibly could. I also wrote songs. Some were from the psalms and some came spontaneously from my heart. My journal became love letters to my Creator.

"He brought me to the banqueting house and his banner over me was love." (Song of Solomon. 2:4)

It has been wonderful to return to some of my journals and see prayers answered in ways I would never have imagined. I also see the progression of my heart's cry, from "Help me, God," to "Use me for Your Glory God." As a child singing *What A Friend We Have in Jesus*, meant He was my friend because the bible told me so. The problem is, until He truly becomes our friend, it is merely words on a page. I bet many of our greatest hymns began as journal entries from those who had laid everything at Jesus' feet because their very lives depended on it. How many times have we left little love notes to our spouse, encouraging him or her with words only meant for each other. There are things I've written only to be read by God.

HOPE is a powerful word. Without it, many people die emotionally, and or physically. Pam and I became close friends. Our home group began to grow. The most important thing was that I was growing on the inside. *"But if we hope for that we see not, then we with PATIENCE wait for it."* (Rom. 8:25)

Renewed strength enabled me to wait expectantly for the miraculous. I was like a little girl waiting for her daddy to come home. He did in unexpected ways. Peace permeated our home. Joy replaced fear. Energy replaced fatigue. He changed me from the inside out NOT the outside in. I have learned that the Lord is more concerned about our maturity than he is about our personal comforts. It is in the valley that we find out what is in our heart, what we truly believe. Life seems to be like a classroom, but who is teaching us? C.S. Lewis said, "There are two kinds of people: those who say to God, "Thy will be done," and those to whom God says, "All right then, have it your way." I love how The Message translation describes hope:

"In alert expectancy such as this, we're never left feeling shortchanged. Quite the contrary--we can't round up enough containers to hold everything God generously pours into our lives through the Holy Spirit!" (Rom 5:5 MSG)

Our marriage grew stronger, but it wasn't easy. I asked myself a lot of "What if" questions. "What if we had waited longer to have children and saved more money?" Or, "What if we had never gone into our own business and Leo remained working for someone else?" "What ifs" are very dangerous in a relationship. Disciplining my thoughts towards Leo was very important. I prayed for him daily. Everyday, my love for him grew. Excitement would fill my heart each time I declared one more blessing. Inserting Leo's name in scripture, I would say, "Everything Leo sets his hand to will prosper." Or "Leo is blessed in the city and blessed in the field." (Deuteronomy 28:3) Or "Leo 'can do all things through Christ who strengthens him.'" (Philippians 4:13) If God spoke the world into existence, obviously, what we speak must reach God's heart. How many times have we felt bad because of something negative or hurtful someone spoke? How many times have we felt better or accomplished more than we could have ever dreamed because of the ENCOURAGING words of someone who cared? If I wanted our family to prosper, I had to CHOOSE to bless Leo during my prayer time. This ended up spilling over into our personal time together. I quit informing him of what I thought he should be doing everyday. My love was no longer conditional, but unconditional. I loved him simply because he was, and continues to be, my husband. I focused on the good things he did, for instance, how affectionate he was with the children and me. Ladies, I am going to speak very candidly. Intimacy was the KEY to affirming Leo's ability to face our issues courageously. We are called to be their lover not their mother. Five kids, one bathroom and three bedrooms was not the most intimate retreat setting for our romance to flourish. If I allowed circumstances or negative feelings to crowd out our time together, I knew Leo's strength would fail. Even if a door of opportunity opened for him, he might not have the courage to walk through it. Many times, I mentally returned to our wedding day. "…for better or for worse, rich or POOR..." There were many days I felt exhausted with very little to offer anyone, let alone my husband. However, on December 28, 1985, we made a vow to 'love, cherish and hold until death do us part.' Remembering those commitments gave me the strength to embrace Leo with open arms. I began to get the feeling Leo's destiny was getting ready to change.

I began to pray specifically for the boys. I believe part of the discipline of prayer is remembering those around us and not taking them for granted. It was easy to meditate on what was giving us immediate stress. It was easier, at times, to meet their needs as best we could and wearily thank God we were all healthy and had survived another day. Bedtime prayers centered on their needs and encouraging them to become all God had for them.

"And he shall go before him in the spirit and power of Elias, to turn the hearts of the fathers to the children, and the disobedient to the wisdom of the just; to make ready a people prepared for the Lord." (Luke 1:17)

Our job is to help our children receive God and His goodness. I believe that many children turn away from God because parents either did not honor God in word and action or they lost heart to heart communication with their child. Every human being has a choice, and some no matter their upbringing have seasons of disappointments and turning away. We must never lose sight of our call to pray for their hearts and destinies.

Alone, I took scriptures and inserted their names in them as well.

"For I know the plans I have for you, Jon, says the Lord. They are plans for good and not for disaster, to give you a future and a hope." (Jer. 29:11)

When I was pregnant with each child, I wanted their names to mean something. I began writing each child's first and middle name in my journal. I would write the meaning of their names and tell them. For instance, I would say, "Christopher, your name means Christ Bearer, or David, your name means Beloved."

"God, if you will give me a son, I will give him back to you." My father, Laban Samuel Magbee was born to Marie and Sidney Magbee soon after. By the time my dad was 26 years old, he was an accomplished violinist and an Atlanta Criminal lawyer. Something kept tugging at his heart. "Mom and Dad, I feel God is calling me to the Ministry." My grandmother told us that for one week following their conversation, the Presence of God filled their home. She remembered her prayer many years before, and the family chose to support him wholeheartedly. Hearing that story as a child, affected me greatly. Could what we do here on earth, affect eternity? God's word says it does.

"For our light affliction, which is but for a moment, works for us a far more exceeding and eternal weight of glory; while we look not at the things which are seen, but

at the things which are not seen; for the things which are seen are temporal; but the things which are not seen are eternal." (2 Corinthians 4:17-18)

God could have called my Dad to be an attorney. Ministry is not always in the confines of the church. We ARE the church, or the Body of Christ. Whether we are in a courtroom or a sanctuary, We are commanded to:

"Go ye into all the world, and preach the gospel to every creature." (Mark 16:15)

Our children began to grow in their gifting. Jon wanted a guitar. He saved $50.00 and purchased one from a friend. While most of the kids were playing outside, he taught himself to play chord progressions through the internet. He spent hours playing in his and the boys' room. Though he played the trumpet, this new instrument had captured his heart. He also began to write songs. David excelled in drumming. I tried to stay sensitive to what they seemed to do naturally. He drummed on tables, chairs, garbage cans. We could not help but encourage him to pursue drumming. The boys were also athletic. They seemed to shine on the baseball field. We have always encouraged the boys to participate in at least one sport. Confidence and sportsmanship is very important to their physical and emotional maturity. We could not afford to throw them into every activity imaginable. We simply watched them create their fun and encouraged them. We have never told our sons what we thought they would do. Like my Dad, God has been faithful in calling them and giving them the gifts they need to accomplish His will. We feel it is our job to make sure they are developing their talents in such a way that God can trust them with His plans and purposes.

"Ree, there is a company that needs your husband." It was the last Friday of our bible study. I never dreamed Pam would speak prophetically at the end of our closing prayer. "OK, God. Do you want me to continue praying for our business?" I asked when I got home. I heard a resounding "No." People may wonder how some hear God's voice. It is usually a still small voice that comes from the Holy Spirit. We were created in God's image. Therefore, we are not just a soul and body. Our spirit is God's dwelling place when we ask Christ into our hearts. This part of our being lives on through eternity. Sometimes it is an impression we feel, or He may speak through a particular scripture that suddenly comes to our mind. Fear and despair caused me to seek the Lord like never before. His voice became clearer and clearer as I faithfully came to Him, seeking wisdom and mercy for our situation.

LADIES, You and I are powerful voices in our home and the world around us. Our sensitive hearts create the very atmosphere we inhabit. Throughout the centuries, the enemy has worked hard to berate us and make us feel weak and powerless. The pain of sexual molestation, divorce, physical abuse, or the world's definition of true beauty have been directly aimed at keeping us buried in our own feelings of inadequacy and unworthiness. Why? We bring forth the very LIFE of creation itself. The seed of humanity is planted deeply within the safety of our womb. A child is born and his or her life is fashioned in the very image of God. The SECRET PLACE of prayer is the PLACE OF POWER. Dreams are birthed in valleys. In the Old Testament there was a great famine in the land. Elijah prayed and continued to send his servant to look for the cloud. His servant would return frustrated. One day, he saw a cloud as big as his fist. Elijah did not look at the ground with feelings of self-pity and remorse. He kept looking up for that cloud that would bring their much-needed rain. Every time he gave orders to his servant to GO and LOOK, he was prophetically speaking to their situation. Those times when nothing seems to be happening, Heaven is waiting for you to SPEAK. Declaring BLESSING over each of your family members RELEASES the Supernatural Power of God on your behalf. Today, YOU are the PROPHETIC VOICE for your family. Take up your weapons and FIGHT for the destiny of you and your loved ones. Victoria Osteen always says, "God is not mad at you. He is madly in love with you!" The Lord, strong and mighty, requests the honor of your presence, so that He may pour healing on your broken heart and restore to you and those around you, what has been lost. AMEN!

"Pastor, I am giving the Beadle family the highest recommendation for this show. It is time for Christians to stand up and receive all God has for them!" Wow. I was speechless. I remembered all the times I stood up in prayer, receiving all God's Word had for my family!

Now, a few short months after that conversation, we are standing in front of lights and cameras. The world was getting a chance to look in on a strong family; a family that had been through tough times and had a story to tell....

Chapter 7

Springs in the Desert

"Hey Guys!" Freddy began. "Whether you win or lose the competition, the producers have chosen you and the kids to represent the show at a press junket in LA." Our mouths dropped. We had to fly out early in the morning and return the next day. We would interview for radio, magazines, newspapers, and television stations. Nervousness took on a whole new meaning. The atmosphere buzzed with excitement and fear as we boarded the plane. There were definite rules concerning what we could and could not say. Approaching the junket was like stepping into another world; a beautiful mansion with a perfectly manicured lawn front and back. It reminded me of an old Elvis movie with the swimming pool in the back yard. (I imagined the King of Rock and Roll playing his guitar near the diving board.) We were escorted to a closed-in porch where there was a food buffet. People were everywhere, all waiting to interview or be interviewed. Several summer reality shows were being introduced. Commercials featuring Leo and the boys played on big screen TVs! We were stunned. "Why are we here?" whispered Leo. My Computer techie husband and I, and five rambunctious boys, were treated like stars. Following a delightful lunch, we were taken to a room in the mansion where a make up artist prepared us for our photography session. "Honey, where are you from?" "I'm from Houston." I replied. Out of the blue, the makeup lady then asked, "Do you go to my favorite preacher's church?" "Might his name be Joel?" I replied. "YES! I watch him all the time!" Here we are at an LA press junket, and my pastor's name is mentioned! She began to share how much hope she felt through his ministry. I knew the reason Leo and I had even stepped out of our ordinary lives to do the show was because our pastor always encourages us to walk through doors of opportunity. We hugged and I encouraged her to come to Houston and visit our church anytime

Pictures were quickly taken prior to our scheduled interviews. First, we were ushered into a huge library with a long table. Each person seated, represented a major radio station. Leo and I sat at one end of the table facing the audience with a microphone placed between us. We were told to answer their questions, but make sure we did not talk at the same time! They wanted to know how Dad Beadle survived my leaving him and the five boys to fend for themselves. We relaxed as they responded with laughter and good will. Our publicity director stood in the background, nodding her head with approval. We had NEVER spoken on radio before, much less in front of a room full of them. A few minutes later, we looked out over the back lawn, to find small awnings lined up in a semi-circle around the entire yard. Each tent represented an NBC network; E!, CNN, Entertainment Tonight, etc. were some of the many we met. Our family was so large; they divided us into two groups. We spent the afternoon interviewing with each network.

We had to be very careful about what we shared because we were simply introducing the show to the press. Feeling very overwhelmed, we attended every interview as best we could. People seemed curious as to how our roles as husband and wife worked. "There are things that Moms do for their families when no one is looking; preparing food the night before; laundry for the next day; sending kisses on their way to school, or holding them when they are hurt. Each spouse brings special gifts to the family. When one is missing, there is a definite void." I shared this many times throughout the day. Leo and I have always had a partnership marriage. Especially facing tough times has caused us to value each other's opinions and advice. We gave some particulars about the different challenges the kids faced. The boys enjoyed telling them how the other family, even though they had girls, was just as competitive as they were. I was very impressed at how positively they spoke of the Clarkson girls, expressing how much fun they had competing against them. After one particular press event, a lady representing a major magazine, walked up to Leo and said, "Your kids were so well-behaved. Whatever you are doing, keep doing it!" I'd written a song about family in case we were asked to sing! At last, one tent was big enough to include all of us. Sure enough, we sang our song: "Thank you for who you are and who I am; we are a family and we will stand. Because LOVE never fails, never fails, never fails..." Once again, our publicity director was beaming. We had decided in the very beginning, that instead of focusing on winning or losing, we would focus on showing people there are strong, thriving families today, and they can have one too. That day, as I watched people observe us from all walks of life, I felt we were fulfilling that desire. As far as I was concerned, our outcome was in God's hands and whichever way it turned out, was fine with me!

"I will open rivers in high places, and fountains in the midst of the valleys: I will make the wilderness a pool of water, and the dry land springs of water." (Isaiah 41:1-18)

Expecting the miraculous is a whole lot different than hoping God will do *something*. Moving from despair to expectation marked the beginning of the miraculous during the hard times. We needed a cool drink of water. During these times of prayer, miracles began to spring up out of nowhere. Driving one car and living in a home that barely fit all of us could have caused us to give up, or think, "This is the way it will always be. Since we are marked for financial struggle the rest of our lives, we'll l try to live as comfortably as possible right where we are." Matthew 9:29 says, *"Then touched he their eyes, saying, According to your faith be it unto you."* Jesus did not heal the blind men because He felt sorry for them, or decided it was a good thing to do; he healed them because of their faith! Notice the blind men did not tell Jesus HOW to heal them; they merely believed He could. HOW Jesus did it, was up to, you guessed it, JESUS! Pastor Joel says, "You may be living in poverty right now, but don't let poverty live in you!" Bankruptcy is not always about finances; relationships can go bankrupt; emotions can go bankrupt. The definition of bankruptcy: "Utter ruin, failure, depletion, or the like." Though the men Jesus healed were physically blind, we can be spiritually blind in our faith. Our souls can walk in total darkness and despair. Just like Jesus healed those men, He can heal our souls so that we can receive all He has prepared for us! God is full of surprises! Springs in the desert represented to me, the miraculous that would totally catch us off guard. I knew there were surprises, but no idea what they would be or how they would happen. If I had known we would one day end up on national TV, I would have tried to figure out how it would happen. That is not the purpose for miracles. Their purpose is to show the world Jesus is alive and well in the hearts of men!

There were many springs in our desert years. While leading worship one Sunday, I felt drawn to a lady in the congregation. I knew I needed to ask her a question. "Marsha, my name is Ree Beadle.," I began. "I know you don't know me very well, but we just moved into a little rent house. My furniture has some stains, and I was wondering if you could advise me on how to clean them." I swallowed nervously, as she responded with a great big smile. "Sure!" she replied. I used to be an interior decorator! I would love to help you in your home." I could not believe my ears. The morning she was to arrive, Leo and I awoke to squishing noises under our feet. Pipes had busted and the floors were saturated in water. Workers arrived to assess the situation. Suddenly, the doorbell rang, and Marsha stood happily at the door. As embarrassment swept over my face, I told her about the water and apologized for any inconveniences. Even though it was wet, she walked in and looked around. "Ree, God is doing something; this happened for a reason. I am going to decorate your home. I have a closet full of wallpaper borders and other items from my decorating days. You will not be in this house for long!" My eyes began to bulge with surprise. "Your family is in a state of transition." she continued, "However, I am going to come everyday and help you decorate." For the next three weeks, Marsha arrived everyday with wallpaper border, flowers, towels, bathroom accessories, etc. Our little home became a cozy retreat from the stress of our circumstances. Each day, she came with an encouraging word. Marsha had been through some difficult financial times due to a previous divorce. Her present husband had been a great blessing and she now walked in prosperity. She told me that during her lonely years, she would always say, "Better days are ahead." That one statement became her statement of faith. She prayed for us every single day. Sometimes, we went shopping or went out for lunch. Several of the items she gave me I still have as a reminder of what a beautiful spring she was.

I had asked God for mentors. He was faithful! Leo and I have always been great friends. However, men need good male role models like those that have gone before them! Leo always says that if you want to know how to fix your sink, don't ask an electrician, ask a plumber! If you want to know how to have a great marriage, ask someone who has one! Ellis Benkenstein loved his wife and was a successful businessman. One of Leo's clients happened to be Marsha's husband! "How are you, Leo?" he would ask. "I mean, how is your marriage? How are your children? How is your business?" He did not want cliché answers! Every time Leo came to work on his computers, Ellis would ask him those same questions. Leo began to open up to him and share his cares and concerns. They prayed together and looked forward to seeing each other on a regular basis. As a matter of fact, Ellis assesses peoples' skills and places them in jobs they would most probably fit. Many times, I found out later, he would tell Marsha, "Leo is not living up to his full potential! He needs to be in a corporate setting." He would give Leo teaching tapes from ministers, encouraging him to seek God and receive His unconditional love. My husband began to change. Our weekly bible studies grew, as he would teach God's Word with renewed strength and trust. We were sensing God was definitely up to something and we were now willing to rest in whatever it was. Leo and I prayed TOGETHER. I tried to help more in the business, and we took more quality time to be with each other.

"Honey, my little car is fixing to die," Leo informed me. "GREAT," I replied. He looked at me with a puzzled expression. "God's Word says, 'he will never leave us nor forsake us!'" Whew! I was actually surprised by my response. "Go get a rental car." Leo replied, "What? How are we going to rent a car INDEFINITELY?" "I don't know," I replied, "but you have to have a car for business, so rent one." Leo tilted his head and said, "Honey, I'll believe with you!" Where did that faith come from? It came from spending time with God and learning to trust Him. I realized at that moment that Leo Beadle was not my sole provider; God was. It was as if chains of fear and worry fell off of me the instant I said, "Great." Excitement filled my heart as we united in faith to believe for the impossible. How were we ever going to obtain two vehicles? They certainly weren't passing out cars on street corners! We also decided not to share our need at church. At this point, God would have to show up without our help! We have learned that JOY is a weapon against fear. It comes from deep within, simply by CHOICE. We had every right to feel afraid. We realized that if God was truly everything I sang and Leo taught, then this was once again, a great opportunity for Him to spring up in our desert. All summer, our boys had piled into our only vehicle to be told later we had no car and would drive a small rental. They watched, as Leo and I went about our days as if everything was fine. Our children watch our actions FAR MORE than listening to our words. "Lord, this is Your time to shine for our kids!" we prayed. The next few weeks were phenomenal.

One Friday night, the phone rang. It was our dear friends, the Harringtons. "I need a truck, so would you guys like to have my Chrysler?" Craig asked. My heart leapt inside! It wasn't a suburban, but it was free. "Absolutely!" I shouted over the phone. Leo happily turned in the rental car and assumed ownership of our 'spring in the desert!' The very next night, the phone rang at 10:00 pm. "Ree, you may not know me, but I am your neighbor and I attend the same church as you." Ok, I thought. So why is she calling me so late at night? "I noticed a large vehicle in your driveway that doesn't look like your car. Your lights are off, so I thought I should call for you to check it out." Wow! People are very protective here! Suddenly, I began to shake nervously. I slowly opened the door, peering carefully outside. She was correct; there was a large blue suburban parked in our driveway but NO ONE was there. I nervously shut the door and ran back to the phone. "Ma'am, you are right! The blue suburban looks like my friend Sonein's!" We hung up, and I called her. "Sonein, is your suburban parked in your driveway?" I quietly asked. "No Ree, I don't own a suburban anymore. It is your suburban and it is parked in your driveway!" I fell to the floor crying for joy as she continued, "We wanted to give it to you last December because we thought we were receiving a big enough bonus to pay it off. However, it didn't happen the way we thought. Recently, my husband received a large bonus that allowed us to give it to you now." I hung up after thanking her over and over again! I ran outside and opened the door. On the seat, there was a note that read: "Hi Beadles! We just want you to know that miracles still happen!" Love, The Noack Family. Another spring in the desert, within a 24-hour period, two vehicles were given to us from two families who lived in two different cities. The Harringtons were our friends from Kinder, Louisiana and the Noacks were our friends and members of our church in Sulphur, Louisiana. Looking back, it was better to receive these gifts after the bankruptcy court date because this suburban was newer than our other one. We drove our cars, both very new to us, as if they were Cadillacs! Miracles tend to come just at the right time! We had been without a family size car since June. It was now October and we had two wonderful vehicles given by two wonderful families.

The Lord began to answer the little desires I had tucked away in my heart. One morning, while talking to God, I told him I wanted my friend Pam to take me to a nearby fancy restaurant. I even went as far as to tell Him I wanted to RIDE in her Jaguar! I actually forgot about it, but a few weeks later, Pam called. "Ree, would you like to go to lunch with me today?" she asked. My heart started pounding. "Yes!" I replied. "You can choose where we go." I told her and then added, "Can we go in your Jaguar?" "Absolutely, we can!" The doorbell soon rang. I opened the door to find her standing there with her keys in the air. "You can drive my car!" My mouth dropped, but I graciously took them from her hand and off we went. I drove as carefully as possible, avoiding any potholes or sudden turns. As we approached the parking lot, I said, "Pam, I want to park away from the other cars to keep it safe." "Ree, it is just a car! And when you see it that way, God will one day give you one!" It was time for another lesson. A jaguar, to her was a blessing, but not the source of her happiness. I learned so much that day. First of all, Pam could have gone to lunch with anyone that day, especially someone who could afford the fancy restaurant. I think it is because Pam's identity is not in riches, but in relationship. She could see my heart and wanted to spend time because she saw my potential! She always spoke and treated me as a friend. She had been through death and knew money did not define her then, and it didn't now. I also learned that God cares about the little details of our lives. He enjoys surprising us with the desires of our heart! Her last words to me that day were, "Tell God what is in your heart, no matter how big or small. Be specific!" Sometimes the embarrassment of our situation causes us to be afraid of forming friendships with people who have more than we do. In actuality, they are the people God sends to encourage us to believe!

Miracles that happen on your behalf are fashioned just for you! That means that when you totally surrender your desert situation to God, your FAITH frees Him to touch your circumstance with His hand of mercy and healing. When I close my eyes, I can picture a barren, dry desert where I am so thirsty and tired. Finally, I cannot move another inch without water. Though fallen to the ground, I look up at the sun. Without warning, water gushes up from the cracks of the dusty ground. I fall onto the thirst-filling springs. I am drenched, after drinking all the water

I can possibly hold. Fullness and contentment fill my body. I roll over and rest. The peace I longed for has been met. That spring in your desert, is Jesus! He is our living water! Just like the woman at the well, Jesus told her He was the Living Water, a well that would never run dry. What did she do after that fateful moment? She ran from town to town telling everyone she had met the Messiah.

I never dreamed while in the desert, we would later end up representing a TV show in LA. Looking out over that luscious green lawn, full of various TV networks, cameras and microphones, I realized this moment was a GIFT. Many of the people were just like us, telling their story and hoping their show would make a difference. I chuckled to myself, thinking, "If they only KNEW what our family has gone through!" However, representing a family TV show, well, nothing could have been more satisfying. We were a team, finally united in purpose for whatever lay ahead. Under the tent, we continued singing, "Together, we face the world, united as one. Together we're never alone; we will overcome." In front of the camera, we sang our simple song about our terrific family.

STREAMS IN MY DESERT

I am hidden in Your praises.
I am safe in Your arms,
Wrapped in Your glory,
Free from all harm.
Tho' 10,000 are at my right side,
All Hell has laid a snare,
There are streams in My desert,
Miracles bursting everywhere.
(By Rena Beadle)

Chapter 8

New Beginnings

The show was airing in one week. "You guys are going to participate in radio interviews via telephone," the publicity consultant stated. We had to gather the family in one room and dial a conference call number. The operator connected us to a particular radio host for a 3-minute question and answer session. "How are we going to talk to someone we can't see?" the kids asked. "We will apply the speaker phone button, so we can all hear him or her at the same time!" Leo replied. We all sat on the floor of our bedroom, waiting for the appropriate time to call; there could be no delays because every minute counted. Looking back, our lives began to take a definite turn of events. The clock was ticking, as our destiny took on a different path. We always thought Louisiana would be our home forever. Our state has never been one that many people moved in and out of unless their company moves them. Cajuns, as we lovingly refer to them, stick together; neighbors become family, where love permeates their homes. They cook the best seafood in the world!

Gumbo is a year round favorite because it's cheap and feeds a lot of hungry mouths. We had just moved into our little rent house, which, thanks to Marsha, was looking better by the day. Like those phone interviews, we didn't know who we would come in contact with or how our lives were fixing to change. We just had to be WILLING to go in a different direction.

One afternoon, I noticed a printed email on the kitchen counter. Curiously, I picked it up and read the message. "Hey Leo, this is your buddy, Kurt Kemmerly! I'm working for a company in Spring, Texas. The boss asked me the other day, if I knew of anyone who could do some of the things he needed accomplished. I told him there is only ONE person I know, and that is Leo Beadle. I told him we used to work together 7 years ago and I highly respect him." Kurt went on to ask Leo if he was interested in a location move at a particular salary. I just stood there. It would well meet our needs! As my heart pounded, I remembered the word Pam gave me at her bible study. Apparently, Leo received the email, printed it, and placed it where I would see it. I ran to the phone and called Marsha. "Do you think this is our miracle?" She calmly replied, "Yes, Ree, I do. Your family has been a great blessing to our church and community. However, you all are not living up to your full potential." I had never really thought about the aspect of potential. I just wanted to get out of this financial mess! We thought the miracles could and would happen right here in Sulphur, LA. While driving around town, Leo and I talked about our possibilities. "Honey, I could sell my business to the competition and go to work for them." My heart sank. "Why? We've received a lot of their customers in the past few years for a reason!" I replied. "I just want to look at all of my options." There he went, ANALYZING the situation. I closed my eyes, took a BREATH, and said, "Leo, pray about it! You will know what we should do." I figured the same ONE who had given me a peace about moving to Texas, would give him the SAME. (I was certainly hoping so!)

Important decisions Leo and I have had to make, once again, remind me of how different we are. I love change! If something isn't working, move on. Sometimes, however, I have acted too hastily. Leo, on the other hand, must process information over time (I bet many of you are nodding your head in total understanding). By this time, however, I'm getting nervous. Would this Cajun ever consider leaving Louisiana? I was afraid of our differences. Once again, I had to go to the secret place. Many of us nod our heads when the preacher says, "God is able to do the impossible!" Sitting in those nice comfortable pews where everybody looks polished and happy, while deep in our hearts, something or someone feels bankrupt in their faith.

"Thy word is a lamp unto my feet, and a light unto my path." (Psalm 119:105)

I pictured a long, winding path surrounded by forest. I saw a man holding a lantern, guiding our family through the long road. The light wasn't so bright we could see for miles ahead; it was just light enough to get us through a mile or so. Every night, Leo and I prayed that God would light our path for His purposes, not ours. There was peace between us. I appreciated the fact that Leo was willing to stay in Louisiana, taking less money, if he felt that was God's will. Fear dissipated, and we both realized whatever was going to happen, it would be for the benefit of our entire family. For some reason, I told God I wanted to go to the interview with Leo! I wanted to meet the owner because of all the experiences with business partners we had in the past. I kind of laughed at my request, especially since I wasn't the one being interviewed, or so we thought.

A phone conversation was set for Leo and his potential boss from Texas. Just like the radio show interviews, Leo was nervous about talking to someone he couldn't meet face to face. Surprisingly, the call lasted 15 minutes. "Honey, I think our conversation went very well! He wants an in-person interview with me and his other Systems Analysts." He paused, "He ALSO wants our entire family to come! He and his family want to take all of us out to dinner after our meeting." My mouth dropped. Leo and I and all five kids were being included. Leo added, "He asked if we attend church, because the interview is Saturday and we will be staying overnight." The man wanted to know if we go to church! Who asks those kinds of questions nowadays? I smiled, and a week later, our plans were set in motion for the first part of

September. My head was in a whirlwind. We gathered the kids together, to discuss the possible career change. They loved their friends and activities. We told them it may or may not happen, but assured them that whatever happened, it would be for all of our benefit. I knew if Leo and I stayed united in our decisions, it would make it easier for them to follow.

Saturday arrived quickly as we piled all seven of us into our car, driving 3 ½ hours to Spring, Texas. Our hotel had plenty to keep the boys busy until Leo finished his meeting. Later, we met at a nearby restaurant for dinner. The owner of the company, and his lovely wife and their three children, met us at the door. Apprehension melted away, as we were introduced with warmth and kindness. Their three children combine with ours, totaled eight kids in all. As we ate, they asked us how Leo and I met, where we were from originally, etc. They also shared their stories, as we laughed and got to know each other better. Jon later recalls, "The boys were getting too rambunctious, so I leaned over to David and said, 'Behave yourselves! Do you want to ruin this for Dad?'" He said that immediately, they sat up straight and grew quiet or QUIETER should I say. He was only 15 years old at the time, yet knew how important this interview was to his father. Later, when the owner followed us back to the hotel, I said, "You really didn't have to invite the whole family, but thank you for allowing us to come!" He replied, "Since our Company is small, it is important to me that we hire happy families. If the spouse is happy, the employee will be also." Leo opened up to him that night, sharing about his business and past bankruptcy. He told us that one of the reasons our business had not succeeded, was because Leo didn't have a product to sell to his customers; Leo sold his services, but he could not duplicate himself. The business was confined to Leo and his own abilities, whereas a product is needed on a regular basis and can be reproduced. We knew one thing; our meeting was not by chance. His job would be to install and support products for community banks all over the nation. There would be traveling, but he would come home at the end of a workweek. Leo understood the banking industry, because he had worked for one during the early years of his career. Servicing customers, well, that was all he did in his own business! It looked like his journey had NOT been in vain. It was merely taking an unexpected turn.

The phone rang 2 days later and Leo got the job! We shouted like two kids at a football game! The catch was that he wasn't going to begin until January: This was September! Mrs. Hyperactivity had to WAIT a little longer. I didn't see much wisdom in that, but as usual, time tells all. Leo had to find someone to take over his business; I had to let the church know I wouldn't be leading worship much longer. To top it off, we had only been in our present house 3 months. I taped a big sign on the front door that read, "Guys, Dad got the job!" As the kids returned from school, everybody jumped up and down, congratulating him; except for little Christopher.

He was in the 5th grade and did not want to leave his friends. We would also be moving at the end of December, a tough time to be changing schools. As time grew nearer, one night I found Jon lying on the couch. "Mom, I'm really going to miss my Youth pastors here!" I was very touched by his feelings. He could have been upset about certain activities or friends he was leaving. He was going to miss them. However, he loved the church LEADERS who had ministered to him week after week. After two going-away parties, I noticed our phone didn't ring as much; grieving friends seemed to pull away. We all had experienced tremendous relationships, but there were no more words to say. Sometimes there are people that cannot emotionally handle when others move on; some can. Entering and leaving is a normal way of life, however, not everyone will be excited because of the pain of letting you go. We gathered the kids together. I told them something I have never forgotten. "Guys, we are not just moving for Dad's benefit. We are moving because there are incredible opportunities for all of us in Houston. Our destiny awaits us as a family! Expect great things." If God was taking us to Houston, He would open doors for all of us.

We had no idea how we could afford Christmas AND move! Once again, Charity was extended, and we received two boxes full of gifts for the boys. As we stood in line, Leo said, "Ree, I truly want to apologize for the last 5 years; it has been very rough, and I am terribly sorry." I looked at him and nodded; there were no words to say. It seemed rather cleansing to have him acknowledge our pain, and take responsibility for it. We both knew it wasn't his entire fault, but humility seemed to heal some of the disappointments and struggles of our past. There are times when saying "I'm sorry," even when it isn't our fault, is very healing to a relationship. How many times do we play the blame game? It was a new day, and we were embarking on a great journey. "Somehow," he continued, "I believe God ALLOWED us to walk through this MESS, so that we can one day share a MESSAGE to others in need of hope." December 28th, 2003, with some help from our friends, we loaded our U-Haul and headed west!

Our friend Gary advised us to rent for 6 months to a year before buying a home. I, Mrs. Anxious, was NOT thrilled about the prospect of another lease. Leo, as usual, was perfectly CONTENT with the idea. Reluctantly, I called an apartment complex and asked for a three bedroom on the ground floor, and near to as many schools as possible. Believe it or not, that is exactly what we got. There were three schools within walking distance from our apartment. Yes, I said apartment! There were 1200 square feet to be exact. All but Jon and Michael (too young) walked. Jon rode the bus. Each child attended his own school. There were a lot of benefits to our living circumstances. First of all, we needed time to pay off some tax debts from our beloved business. Secondly, we needed time for our credit scores to increase before we purchased a home. Waiting, as you can tell, has never been my forte! What began as a six month lease, turned into a 1 ½ year lease. Most of the families came and left after six months, either building a home, or looking for one. My dream of owning had to be placed on the back burner. I kept telling myself I needed to be happy for those that could move on so quickly! I realized that it took time to go bankrupt and it would take TIME to recover. One of the benefits of apartment life was FREE repairs. There was always a handy man on site. It was a good thing, because a few weeks after moving in, a pipe burst and water gushed out from the ceiling on to our kitchen table!

Christopher did not want to go to school his first day. I took his hands and we bowed our heads and prayed that even though Chris was sad, God would lead him throughout his day and bless him. He did just that. The lady in charge of registration was from Louisiana. She had a long chat with him, sharing some of her memories as he sat attempting to smile. The school had an Ambassador program for new students, where a child was chosen by his or her class to accompany a new person throughout the school day for one week. The Ambassador would walk the child to class, as well as eat with him or her in the cafeteria, introducing the student to their classmates. Chris walked away grinning ear to ear, as the young man walked with him to class. I was relieved. Once again, GRACE met us in our time of need. The emotional well-being of our sons has always been important to us. Happy children have a larger capacity to transition to the different phases of their lives than those who are lonely or depressed. I knew Chris would go through a grieving process, but I wanted to make sure he was passing THROUGH the sadness, NOT remaining there. Counseling can be extremely helpful for kids who seem to struggle with change. Talking to someone can be very healing to a wounded heart.

Our friend, Gary Babineaux, once again, offered some advice: "Go to Lakewood Church." "Ree, you can go to a smaller church and be IT musically, OR you can go to Lakewood and there will be greater resources for your children to be developed!" I believe that God places in the church who He wants. For us, I believe his advice was prophetic. The first time we visited Lakewood Church, Leo told me, "This is where God wants us." Love enveloped the atmosphere as the congregation sang, "I am a friend of God…" The choir was incredible as the worship leader led the very songs I had led in Louisiana the last few years. Her music changed my heart and those in our church. Cindy Cruise Ratcliff was, and still is, an incredible inspiration to my family and me. It was a great honor to be able to attend the very church whose music had comforted and encouraged us through difficult times. The size of the congregation and building was quite overwhelming at first. Immediately, we sought an adult Sunday school class to meet other couples. Fortunately, we joined a Marriage class. We began to make friends. The children attended Children's' Church and Youth Group. Once again, we had found a new church home. It was amazing how the largest church in America became small as we met new friends and volunteered in ministry.

One day, Leo received a post card in the mail. Somehow, a company knew we had filed Chapter 7; it was an invitation to a Bankruptcy Seminar. The most enticing part about it was the conference was FREE. Leo and I decided to go. As we pulled up to the hotel parking lot, there were parking signs that only read SEMINAR. We entered a large ballroom, full of people. We didn't know what to anticipate, but we were open to any advice on bankruptcy recovery. We sat at long tables facing the front of the room, where a big movie screen scrolled down to the floor. The gentleman speaking on the video was Steven Snyder. Apparently, he and his wife had fully recovered from bankruptcy years before and were sharing how they did with others such as us. They work with local businesses in each city to provide helpful tips and services to those in recovery. The first thing we had to do was stand, turn to the stranger next to us, and declare, "Hi, I'm Ree Beadle and I'm bankrupt." At first, we were taken back by that request. I felt like we were at an AA meeting! It had been several years since we filed and I didn't see myself that way anymore. But, we were still recovering from the financial trauma of those previous years. Before we knew it, we were laughing and hugging the people around us. It was actually rather FREEING; it made the shame of our past less overbearing. Suddenly, we knew this seminar was part of our new beginning. God was giving us a game plan for our future. The information we learned was invaluable and will be shared later in the book.

Pastors Joel and Victoria Osteen are known around the world as Ministers of hope. Week after week, they encourage people to trust God. Joel always says, "Start expecting the unexpected." Circumstances had definitely driven us to that point already, but were there more for us? Leo loved his new job, and the kids were adjusting to their new schools. Our pastor also quotes the psalms, when he says, "The path of the righteous gets brighter and brighter." I couldn't shake the feeling that there were more opportunities ahead. 1Cor. 2:9 says, *"No man has ever seen or heard or even imagined the wonderful things God has in store for those who love the Lord."* I wanted to join the Music ministry, but with Leo's new job and five kids in four different schools, it wasn't the right time. Once a month, Leo traveled. That may not sound like a lot to some, but having five kids in four different schools living in a 3-bedroom apartment was plenty! My days were full. We were meeting new friends and enjoying our new church. Pastor Joel also teaches us to remember daily the good things God has done. We enjoyed our marriage class. As time passed, the Sunday school leaders began to call on us to share our testimony. Following a panel discussion, a lady walked up to me and asked me if I would like a job in advertising for a local newspaper. I didn't even read the newspaper, nor had I even thought about working, much less full time!

My resume mainly consisted of Music Ministry. The Editor glanced at it as we laughed for about an hour. I was then offered the job as an Advertising Consultant. Basically, I sold advertising to small local businesses. The employees watched me, especially since I had absolutely no experience in this field! There was one thing I did know – People. I went door to door, passing out the weekly newspaper and offering ad services. I enjoyed meeting business owners and employees of every career. My sales increased, as relationships were formed. I started holding Networking luncheons where instead of having special speaker, business owners could come and share what they did and where they were located. I had actually grown more confident because of the years I helped Leo. I was definitely not as afraid of failing as I used to be. Sometimes, I wondered how I managed working full time, five boys and a husband who traveled a lot. However, it was because of that newspaper, I found out about the reality show. By the time filming began, one of my customers hired me on a part-time basis as a Director of Education for a tutorial company. Once again, I had to learn new skills. My journey had taken some unexpected turns, yet I can look back and appreciate every moment. I thought moving to Houston would mean immediately jumping into Music Ministry. Instead, I was taking leaps outside of my comfort zone -- loving and hating every minute of it. Pastor Joel said, "Jesus told the disciples, 'You can't put new wine in old wine skins.' He was saying you can't go to a new level with an old way of thinking. For something new to happen, something has to resonate on the inside. It's time to give God permission to increase you! If it's a little cup, it's time to get rid of that!

You might think a barrel is big, but get rid of that, too! God has a barn-load full of blessings in store for each one of you." Live Like A Champion and "Increase your capacity to receive." It felt really good! New beginnings for us meant change in every area of our lives; location, church, home and schools. If we are willing, God strategically gives us a new heart that can handle those new beginnings.

There in our bedroom, we were getting ready to talk with radio hosts we could not see. We spoke with people across the Nation. We were ready. Our family sat still, intently listening to each person, quietly waiting for our turn to share. We didn't want to miss what he or she was saying. I think that is the way we should be with God; always listening and alert to what He may be speaking. Just like the radio interviews, when the host speaks, we must respond. God is waiting for us to be still and listen. He is ready to speak!

Chapter 9

Back to Basics

As is typical during ball season, we were playing baseball games. While at the ball field, we, meaning Leo and the boys received another chore. We guys had to throw a pool party the very next day. This meant we had to purchase a pool, assemble it and invite ten guests. As soon as the ball games were over, we headed to the store . We headed back to our apartment and began working. All of a sudden, my son Jeremy came outside holding a bare coat hanger with a note on it, saying: you have to shop. Shop? For what? "There are no towels or sheets or clothes in the house," Jeremy says. I go look in disbelief and check. He was right. There was not a stitch of clothing hanging in the closet or in the drawer. There was not even a face towel, not a dishtowel, nothing in the apartment as far as towels, linens, clothes -- nothing. The beds were completely stripped except for the mattresses on box springs. The chore said we had to go buy all new linens, clothes and out fit your entire house, your entire family for the rest of the week. Great, this is EXACTLY what I, Leo, wanted to do. Shop! The worse thing I could think of doing: shop. Meanwhile, we are still trying to put a pool party together. Needless to say, we were very busy. All we had were the clothes on our back, and for some of my kids, it consisted of baseball uniforms and cleats.

We finally got the pool assembled and began filling it with water. I finally asked where we were going to shop and they told me it was JC Penney's. Great, there was one in the mall. Sorry. The one we had to go to was at another mall forty-five minutes away. Yikes! We were already on a tight time-line and now we had to add an hour and a half or more of travel to that. I shrugged my shoulders and packed the kids in the van and off we went. Upon arriving at the store, the first thing they told me was that I had to separate myself from the kids and buy a complete outfit for each of the boys without them being with me. They knew how challenging this would be for a man. I don't do the shopping for the kids. I ended up buying them shoes that were two sizes too big, belts that were three times longer than they should be, baggy clothes or those that were too tight. It was kind of funny, but it was all for the show. I didn't realize how much Ree did for us, just how much she knew about the boys; how big their feet were and things I just took for granted. We spent several hours, allowing even the boys to go on their own shopping spree. About two hours into this chore, I suddenly realized I hadn't shopped for myself. I was too busy getting linens for the beds and towels for the bathrooms and dishtowels for the kitchen. Here it is, nine o'clock at night and I haven't bought anything for me; new tennis shoes, new dress shoes and dress slacks for church and clothes for the next week. I was exhausted. As the store workers were helping us get our stuff out the door with multiple flat beds of merchandise, I was wondering HOW we were going to fit all of this AND the kids in the VAN. We managed to stuff it all on top of the kids and under the seats. Then we headed back to the apartment. It was way past our bedtime, but we had to put make beds and put towels and clothes up and on and on and on. As I fell in the bed that night, I wondered, "What will tomorrow hold?"

Going through this experience really reminded me of going through the bankruptcy. We had to go back to the essentials or basics of life. It meant going back to our foundation, the simplest, most fundamental principles. It forced us to question everything we thought was so important. Every THING in our life. I have learned that over time we add comforts that only bring more work and frustration. One resolve I have come to through this experience is that I want a simpler life. In a world full of commercialism and high technology, our lives can become so cluttered we lose sight of what is really important. I thought of this during the show, in the apartment, void of any clothes, and nothing in the apartment except furniture and me and my kids. It brought me back to what is the simplest common denominator of life: family, our most valuable asset.

Getting back to basics in any situation is a choice. Going through a bankruptcy will definitely strip you down to the brass tax. We walked away with clothes, a couple of older cars and ourselves. There was nothing left to our name. Now, since we have been adding back to our lives, I think we are far more careful to only add that which truly enriches our lives and doesn't just add clutter. By no means are we perfect at this. After all, we are just human. One example is the pool table in our game room. We bought it because we "needed" it. We've had it for several years and it's primary use is a table that collects junk. Will we ever learn?

You may have heard it before but we need to have our priorities straight. How do we do that? I think we have to let the Lord examine our hearts and speak to us. After all, the scripture teaches us that He alone truly knows what is in the hearts of men. Therefore, we need to seek His priorities and let Him guide us in jettisoning the priorities that are not of Him and accept His grace to embrace the priorities that are His design. This requires some real death to self and to what we see on TV. Remember Madison Avenue makes their living by tricking us into buying into the lie that "we have to have it", whatever the "it" is. Be strong and of good courage and learn to say "no" to your flesh and walk in God's spirit. It is freeing beyond belief.

Once we've begun making the hard decisions in our life and are reining in our spend-thrifty habits we can start digging out of the debt hole. Here are some things we have learned through our plunge into bankruptcy and rise from the pit with God's help. First, get a job! That's right you need a steady income. Both spouses may have to work if needed. Fundamentally, we have come to loath debt. The Word of God has some very dire warnings about the subject. However, when you have gone down to nothing you may still need some form of credit worthiness to do something as simple as rent an apartment. Here are some things we learned from others about this. Protect your credit score. Learn what lowers and what raises it. Raising your credit score means paying your bills early or on time! Do not use more than half of your available credit. Only keep two or three credit cards, closing those with the smallest credit limits. Allowing creditors to pull your credit report often will definitely lower your score. Instead, when purchasing a car for instance, YOU pull your three credit reports and scores(the scores are separate from the reports) ahead of time. This does not lower your credit. While you are at the dealership, give the financial manager your basic information minus permission to pull your credit reports until a price agreement is made and they "pre-approve" you based on what you've shown them. Then you give them permission to pull your credit report so they can verify the information you gave them is correct.

I would also advise against trying to buy a home right out of the gate. Take a year or two to rebuild your credit by doing the "right" things that help raise that score. Secondly, if you have drivable and repairable vehicles I would put off replacing them for 3 or 4 years if possible. It is actually easier to buy a home than a car. This has been our experience. Start saving money so you can put down a decent down payment if not pay cash for a good used car.

We also learned that hiring a professional advocate to dispute negative credit information on our credit reports can many times result in the removal of entries that have lowered your credit score. We got one of the bureaus to drop our bankruptcy just a few months after it was discharged. Even if you don't hire someone, you can dispute mistakes yourself. The law entitles you to receive all three credit reports once a year for free. Just go to http://www.annualcreditreport.com or call toll-free 877-322-8228. To get your credit scores you will need to pay for them but this usually costs less than thirty dollars for all three.

If you have outstanding business debt especially in the form of back taxes owed we can tell you first hand that hiring a good CPA to talk with the taxing authorities is a great idea. It will not only de-stress you but they can often negotiate a settlement for less than you owe or at the very least negotiate a payment plan you can live with. Our CPA did wonders for us.

Another aspect of going back to basics is taking stock of your relationships. Are the people you are hanging around just 12 months behind you on the journey to bankruptcy? Are they suffering from the same pitfalls that plague your life? If so, you need to find some new friends. Your close friends are a very big part of life and we need to value and cherish them. However, we must guard against poisonous or damaging relationships. Sometimes you may come across people in your path that may not be good for you. They may be distractions from the plans and purposes of your life. We let someone into our inner circle of friends we shouldn't have, and now we have a problem because they know they are in your inner circle and it's hard to get them out. This is not grade school or High School; this is life. When we let someone come into our inner sanctum of friendship, it needs to be someone that adds to our lives, not subtracts; someone who is enriching our lives; someone with which there is a mutual growth happening between us.

We have to value our heart enough to guard against unhealthy relationships. If there is someone that does not belong in our lives, we need to get rid of them. That sounds mean and ugly. I don't mean to imply that you have to be harsh, but remain selective when it comes to close friendships. You can still be kind but not afford certain people opportunities to be with you. God can show you how. Just ask Him. Remember, we are not saying that these are bad people. They just may be bad for you! Everyone is loved by God, but not everyone is right for you. These might be relatives or people you serve beside in everyday places. The Holy Spirit will help you cultivate relationships with people who will help you become all God created you to be. Not only do you need to rid yourself of the wrong people in your life but you also need to begin to seek after the right people for you. We all need those who act as mentors in our lives because they are beyond us spiritually, emotionally and financially. There are a few people I trust to speak into my life because they are further along than where I am now. They are where I want to be, and in the place God has called me to go. They can tell me anything and question me on everything. Because I know God has placed them in my life and they are trustworthy sources that genuinely love and care for me, they have permission to impart into my life. Most people I know do not, nor should they have this amount of freedom with me. It has to be the same in your life. When you consider allowing someone into your close confidence, ask yourself if God has brought him or her or is this person a distraction? You should always be at peace with the people in your inner circle. Where there is confusion, there is no peace. When there is no peace it is time to make some relationship changes.

When we came home from the ball field and found everything missing, I was in total shock. They gave us four thousand dollars in the form of gifts cards to shop at JC Penney as fast and furious as we could. We had 2 ½ hours to replace everything we needed. I did not have time to think about what I would LIKE to have. After the show ended, Ree couldn't believe I only spent twenty-five hundred of the four thousand dollars we were given. I was just trying to get our basic needs so we could SURVIVE the rest of the week. I had always been the type of person that put everybody else's needs ahead of mine, sometimes to a fault. It was difficult simply choosing what I needed, let alone, what I wanted. God had provided an abundant blessing but in my small mindedness I restricted the size of the blessing. When God blesses us we need to take in all He has for us and not short change ourselves!

I needed to know God's basic plans for managing money. God's Word has plenty to say about finances. His rules govern not only the heavens but the financial realm as well.

There are rules God has placed in this creation about how finances operate and how we must operate them. His rules include putting God first in giving. We cannot violate this if we are to prosper. Proverbs 22:7 says " the borrower is slave to the lender". It repeatedly warns against the use of debt. How can we ever assume debt won't cost us anything? We used debt to rescue us, and it did just the opposite. It enslaved us. It was easy to use credit cards again once we moved to Houston. School and sports activities are much more expensive than Louisiana, so we foolishly encountered some extra debt. Periodically, we have had to go back to basics. Dave Ramsey's material has been extremely helpful in getting us back on track. He helps people to not only get rid of credit card debt, but mortgages as well. Dave says that when you do not have debt, you have options. The world wants us to have everything right now, but if you delay and save money to purchase something, there is much more freedom.

Moreover, just as God has rules governing financial matters, the reality show had very definite rules for what could and could not be purchased. For instance, the kids could not buy any clothes that had labels on them. The only thing they wore that could have logos was their underwear because no one could see that on TV! The show rules, like God's financial rules could not be broken. There were people who constantly watched us, to make sure we were following their guidelines. If we broke a rule, they stopped and corrected us immediately. Ree and I must be the referees for our finances, not allowing each other to break rules we've set for getting out and staying out of debt. The Bible and a budget are the rules we have set to govern our life.

If you are starting over, my message for you is never to lose heart. God took us from the pit of nothingness and blessed us with a beautiful home in a wonderful city. He is faithful, but you have to do it His way. Ree and I sometimes thought we did not even want to live another day. Crises can make people think unhealthy thoughts. There is NO EXCUSE for us to die physically or spiritually when the winds are blowing. Jesus is the same yesterday, today and tomorrow. Let God be God. Instead of ending our lives or running away, we CHOSE to change and grow. It was a very simple decision; taking responsibility for our actions and moving on. This is the route our children and grand children need us to take. Despite any mistakes we may have made, the people around us are moved more by our courage than failures. I read recently that a man who had been a child star, recently tried to commit suicide because his wife left him and they lost everything to bankruptcy. Thank God he didn't die. I remember feeling my family would be better off without me; but deep within my heart, I knew Jesus paid the price for our pain. We don't have to die; He already did! If our lives or marriage had ended due to our pain, our children would not be where they are today. We would not be helping OTHERS stay married, either.

Back to the show, I, Leo, never had shopped like that before. I learned a lot about myself that day. I realized just how little I did in the way of domestic spending. I brought home the bacon, but knew little about providing for my own clothes, let alone the boys. I felt like a fish out of water. I had to change in order to complete the challenge. Today, I am more willing shop and share those responsibilities with Ree. I had to be willing to do things that were uncomfortable so I could accomplish each challenge successfully. Today, I must continue to change in order to become the man God wants me to be. I've chosen to embrace the change that comes with doing God's will.

Chapter 10

Treated Like Royalty

Saturday morning began early. It was time for breakfast while dinner's gumbo simmered on the stove. The kids sat down to eat, and we were feeling good, even if cameras WERE in our faces the entire time. I had been to the grocery store the day before, with a list of meals for the next two weeks. That is reality for us because I buy groceries twice a month. I write down all the meals we are going to eat, and make sure the necessary items are purchased. It cuts down on unnecessary spending. (I also usually go shopping ALONE without little hands placing extras in the cart!) I felt very confident that with my careful attention to running the household, along with everyone's help, we had a great chance to win this game. Breakfast consisted of scrambled eggs, TURKEY bacon (reason given later), fruit and milk. We also did not forget our vitamins!

An unexpected knock at the door, startled me. Reality show or no reality show, 9am on a Saturday morning was early for visitors. Still in my pajamas, I reluctantly answered the door. A tall gentleman in a business suit handed me a scroll, and announced, "Mom, this is just for you." I thanked him and shut the door. Still smelling of gumbo, eggs and bacon, I was NOT prepared for what was fixing to happen. Gathering the family together, I unrolled the very long parchment and began reading: "Mom, look around you. You have a happy home, beautiful children, a loving husband, and a busy, wonderful life. You are the glue that holds the family together. You make it look easy, but no one works harder than you. We want you to know you are appreciated. In fact, we think you need a break, so we're taking you to a place where there are no responsibilities. For the rest of the week, your hectic schedule will be replaced with blissful, pampered relaxation and exciting adventures…because you are leaving your family behind! Dad, you must become Mister Mom. You have to take care of the kids, stay on schedule and try to win the game without your wife's help. Mom, you've got fifteen minutes to pack and give Dad all the advice he'll need to get him through the week…" Tears filled my eyes as I tried to finish reading. "Am I going on a vacation?" I asked Leo in disbelief. "Yes honey, you ARE." I continued reading: "You've got 15 minutes to pack and give Dad all the advice he'll need to get him through the week. Your fifteen minutes start NOW, so hurry the clock is ticking!" I jumped up, gave orders to the family, and headed to the shower. Glancing at our weekly menu, Leo asked," How do I make cornbread casserole?"

"Cornbread mixes, eggs, milk, stir together. Pour half in casserole dish. Brown grown meat and add taco seasoning. Pour beef on top of mix, add grated cheese, then top it with the rest of the cornbread mix and THROW it in the oven at 350 degrees. THAT'S IT." I finally lowered my hands from demonstrating as I spoke. Leo stood there scratching his head, while I ran to the bathroom. I had fifteen minutes to prepare for where? The boys, trying to be helpful, threw my suitcase on the bed, shouting, "Mom, hurry up! You'll be disqualified if you're LATE." They couldn't help me pack because they are boys.

I ran out the door, suitcase in hand and a towel wrapped around my wet head. I figured that wherever they were taking me, I had plenty of time in the vehicle to put my make up on and beush my messy hair. Suddenly, I was greeted by the same gentleman I'd met earlier that morning. He helped me into a beautiful gold Armada SUV. While waving good-bye to my still very bewildered family, I nervously climbed inside. "Mom's just going to church." said four-year-old Michael to one of the producers. Still shaking, I was sitting in a car, going somewhere I didn't know, while a producer holds a camera to my not-made-up face. "How do you feel about leaving your family?" he asked. I could hardly reply, as once again, tears welled up in my eyes. All I could think about was how this whole show idea was MINE. Now, the entire competition was up to the kids and Leo, AKA MR. MOM. I replied, "I need a BREAK." My head fell back and I started laughing. "Where do you think you are going?" the producer asked. "I don't know; maybe to a spa in downtown Houston for a couple of days." I replied. It sounded good to me. At that instant, I decided to enjoy this unexpected journey, WHEREVER it was. Our interview continued as the car suddenly turned towards Bush Intercontinental Airport. I started shaking again. "I'm n-n-not going downtown Houston." I exclaimed. Now I REALLY had to brush my hair! "Hand me your cell phone please." What? Why did he need my cell phone? Trembling, I handed it to him, knowing I was giving away my only communication with my family. The car stopped at the airport drop-off. Everyone got out of the car except me and the driver. I grabbed my makeup bag, preparing to leave. "Ma'am," the gentleman quietly spoke, "I've never met you before, but I've been greatly touched by what you shared in the car on the way here. I hope that wherever you are going it will be wonderful." He then opened the door for me to exit. Approaching the airport gate, I concluded that it was truly meant for Leo and the boys to play the game without me. Obviously, it was meant for me, Rena Beadle, to relax, something I hadn't done in a very long time.

We were bound for San Antonio. "We," meant me and the entourage of cameramen who accompanied me to our final destination. I hadn't flown First Class in years. It felt good, even though it was a short flight. I sat unscrambling all the thoughts running through my mind. "How are the boys reacting since my departure?" or

"Where could I possibly be staying?" "How is the family going to make it without me?" I believed I was the most prepared for the show because I had done almost ALL of the preparation work. It dawned on me that my pre-show participation was planned all along; it kept Dad from being in the spotlight until the APPOINTED time of my DEPARTURE. "Mrs. Beadle, you are going to LOVE this resort," the producer exclaimed, as we approached a big stone gate that read Hyatt Hill Country Resort. "GREAT, because I've NEVER been to one," I replied. He drove me down a long road surrounded by trees on either side. We finally approached a beautiful ranch-style hotel. My heart POUNDED at the thrill of the elegance of this paradise. To top it off, it was obviously planned just for ME. I felt like a young girl, looking in wonder at such beauty; knowing it was for REAL. All the hours I had spent the past few months getting ready for the show paled in comparison to the splendor of my new surroundings. The car stopped at the circle drive in front of the entrance. I was escorted into the lobby. My mouth dropped, as my eyes took in the breath taking grandeur of my new home-away-from-home. The Western charm seemed to welcome me with open arms. All I had to do was receive this beautiful gift and enjoy each minute. Henry David Thoreau said, "Our truest life is when we are in our dreams awake."

I was finally ushered to a suite, complete with a living and dining room. Fresh flowers were everywhere. Sitting on the couch was a familiar looking lady. I gasped. "You must be Terry, are you?" Terry Clarkson, our competition's mom quickly rose to meet me. We were hugging and laughing like old friends. We sat down together, shaking our heads at the thought of our husbands running the households without us. "I just don't think Leo can cook rice!" More laughter followed. We were going to share our week TOGETHER. A little while later, we were whisked away on a tour of our new get-away. Memories of cooking, cleaning and chauffeuring kids quickly faded away in the light of our new surroundings. We felt like ROYALTY. Green, Luscious Texas hills gave way to golf courses, bike paths and swimming pools. Dinner was served outside, as we shared stories about what it was like raising five boys and five girls. For instance, I was totally shocked to discover Terry ironed some of the girls' hair. That is one thing I didn't have to worry about. "I wonder what they are wearing," she asked. I smiled, thinking that was the FURTHEST thing from my mind. I told her I just hoped the boys kept their ROOMS clean. Laughter continued. I learned Terry and Henry Clarkson had a strong marriage. We also shared similar concerns about raising kids in today's world. We each had at least one teenager at the time. It was nice to realize she cared as much about their future as I did mine. We talked about how difficult it was at times to communicate with our kids as they got older. We did not want to feel isolated from them. We decided that our focus would be to show the world there are STRONG, happy families. There are those that choose not to divorce because they've grown 'out of love'. We were in our marriages for forever. More similarities included the fact that we disciplined our kids, attended church on a regular basis, and believed being a mom was the highest calling any woman can have. Even if someone cannot have children, mothering extends beyond the four walls of our homes. There are many people that need a mom in their lives. That too, is an incredible gift. We had no idea what we were going to be doing that week, but it was going to be a lot of fun sharing it with my new friend.

The next morning, once again, I awakened to a day full of surprises. "Lord, THANK YOU for bringing me to this beautiful place." A knock at the door revealed a chef inviting us to help him cook breakfast in our dining room. We giggled as he taught us how to cook eggs, bacon and French toast all at the SAME time. As we finally sat down to eat, much to our surprise, closed circuit TV came on. Speechless, we got to see some of the activities our families had already encountered, as well as their emotional responses to our absence. Terry's younger daughters had tears running down their faces, as they watched the van whisking her away. Looking totally bewildered, I watched the boys give dad high fives like they were fixing to play baseball or something. Terry and I did not know whether to laugh or cry! We had only been gone 24 hours, and already the competition was in full swing. There was no time to worry, because WE were visiting the SPA. Riding in a golf cart, we approached what appeared as a renovated barn. It was surrounded by beautiful flowers and soft music playing in the background. We walked in to a store filled with lotions, soaps and other various toiletries. Escorting us to a dressing room complete with robes and sandals a lady said, "Please put these on and wait here until your name is called" We sat in a smaller waiting room in the back, drinking as much juice as we wanted. Eventually, I was taken to a small room, where the massage therapist waited for me. The stress of all the excitement melted at the touch of her fingertips. The hour seemed only a few minutes. I did not want this moment to stop, however following my treatment, Terry and I were allowed to relax on lawn chairs outside. Lunch was served in the quiet surroundings of our peaceful environment. The atmosphere, once again, stilled my anxious thoughts. Entering the salon for a cut and color, I noticed the hair stylist seemed nervous. I encouraged her to relax. "You must be yourself. You will have a greater chance of making it on TV." I explained. Acting is not wanted on a reality show; being you is. We had a great time as she gave me a new, fresh look.

We had an awesome lady producer, who made sure our pampering was done with perfection. She even took time to make my face after my hair was done. My princess heart glowed in the aftermath of my special day. I felt like a young girl again without a care in the world. I was surrounded by people whose only concern was to make my vacation as comfortable as possible away from my normal hectic life. Every woman desires to be treated as if she was the only woman on earth. I felt like a costly treasure.

I didn't think life could get much better than this. I wondered how Leo and the kids were doing. I knew it must be stressful without Mom. Maybe they were better off without me. Once again, I turned them over to God and focused on what was going on around me; chefs cooking beautiful delicacies for our culinary fill; my bed was turn down every night with mints on the pillow. Activities were arranged and we simply arrived. There was no one else except me and the other mom. One day, we took Salsa lessons at the San Antonio River Walk. Adorned in Spanish attire, I was whirled around an open-air stage as if I was a famous guest dancer. The sun beamed down on my smiling face, as if God was saying, "I have turned your mourning into dancing...." Every night, I returned to my room, finding gourmet chocolate decorating fine china. One evening in particular, there were three waffle cones dipped in chocolate, filled with berries; black berries, blue berries and raspberries. The plates themselves had chocolate decorated in circular motions under the cones. That night, I dozed off, relishing the thought of what the next day would bring.

The next morning, I spotted what looked like a hatbox, or an old looking traveling case. The producer had asked me, before the show ever started, to write down a list of things I would love to do, but never had the chance. One of them was ice-skating. I opened the lid, to find a beautiful little pair of ice skates and a long purple boa. I was definitely enchanted. However, as always, I never knew what to expect. Terry and I anticipated ice skating lessons in a girlie fashion. Wrong. We were taken to an ice rink. Who was at the ice rink was a total surprise! There were two professional ice hockey players. We were taken to their locker room, where our ice hockey team uniforms were administered. The only way to describe it was that we looked like football players with ice skating shoes. For the next hour, these hard working gentlemen tried desperately to teach us how to ice skate while handling hockey sticks. They pushed and pulled us up and down that rink, until Terry and I both fell down laughing HYSTERICALLY. Towards the end of our crazy afternoon, our instructors said, "Ree, since you didn't get to take regular ice skating lessons, we want you to experience flying through the air." What? They hooked a bungee chord to the backside of my belt. Here I am, wearing some 6-foot something professional hockey player's uniform, trying to leap as they pull on the chord. I tried and tried, but for the life of me, could not get my feet off the ground! It was a lot safer dancing the Salsa at the River Walk, but definitely not as funny.

One night, we were given the evening off. Choosing the steak restaurant in the hotel, Terry and I sat eating and sharing our experiences thus far. While we were reminiscing, the chef appeared, just to say HI. When does a chef leave his kitchen just to say hi? No one has ever done that for me before. Besides, with so many children, neither Terry nor I spend much time in fancy restaurants, let alone being visited by the chef. The menu I left for my kids definitely did not measure up to the food I had eaten the past few days. I was convinced we were the most important guests in that hotel. If we weren't, we had no idea.

While Leo and the boys wondered when I was coming home, I FORGOT which day it was. I had no way of communicating with the outside world. They had even taken the phones out of our hotel rooms. I did get to see their pool party on closed circuit TV, but I couldn't help them at all. They looked like they were having a great time, but I had no way of really knowing. I couldn't even offer advice. It actually felt really good. They were in God's hands and that was fine with me. We needed the prize money, but I didn't want to focus on the outcome and miss this incredible experience. How many times do we worry about what we cannot do? This trip convinced me that taking one day at a time is a very important part of life's lessons.

My mind later drifted to the fairy tale Sleeping Beauty. Once upon a time, there was a king and queen who celebrated the christening of their first-born child. The fairies in attendance, spoke blessings over her, as they gathered to celebrate at the great feast. They said the princess would be the loveliest creature in the world, intelligent, graceful, dance perfectly, sing beautifully and play many kinds of instruments. It was a perfect afternoon, or so they thought. Evil lurked around the corner. Unbeknownst to the royal family, a witch quietly entered. The evil creature suddenly announced that if the princess pricked her hand with a spindle, she would die. One of the fairies, though not able to totally annul the curse, proclaimed that if the princess pricked her finger, she would not die, but sleep for one hundred years. As a matter of fact, everyone in the palace would sleep. Sure enough, sixteen years later, the princess priced her finger on the spindle and she and the entire palace fell asleep. For the next one hundred years, people tried to approach the castle, hearing rumors of those who had fallen asleep. No one could penetrate the forest even to approach the castle. At the right time, the prince came looking for her. The forest immediately opened for him to pass through, because 'a real prince is always brave.' He was appalled to find the entire household asleep. As he opened a door, there lay the princess. He was taken by her beauty and bent down to kiss her soft face. Her eyes began to flutter, as she arose to discover who had awakened her. Their eyes met for the first time, as she responded to his love. For so many years, in the midst of diapers, formula, five kids and bankruptcy, my dreams lay sleeping. My experience at the resort awakened those desires like a seedling popping up from deep within the ground. If this wonderful surprise could happen, what else was God capable of doing? I was coming alive. Not only did the princess awaken, but those around her did as well. I felt the kids were affected by our courage simply to do the show. Whatever the outcome, we knew the experience would always encourage them to dream. There is no end to our destiny when we walk in faith.

Wednesday morning, I was served breakfast in bed. I noticed Terry was eating in her room, so I grabbed my tray and tiptoed to her room. We sat on her bed laughing and eating like two little schoolgirls. As usual, there was a knock at the door. The cameramen went to my room first, but I was not there. Rather perplexed they looked towards the dining area and spotted me in Terry's ROOM. Here they came, laughing at us. "We didn't feel like eating alone," we told them. They announced, "This is your last day," they said. Our mouths dropped. "Finish eating because you will then have fifteen minutes to pack and get ready for the rest of your day." Oh no, not another time schedule! "One more thing -- you gals cannot talk to each other until it is time to leave." What did she just say? Two women spending the day together, not to mention the last five days, could not say another word? Ouch. We didn't have much time to think because we had to pack our bags. My suitcase was definitely not as full as Terry's. Her five daughters helped her pack for the trip. She had sweaters, blouses, several pairs of pants and shoes. I had to borrow a jacket from her at one point! Sadly, she and I hugged and silently approached the spa for our last day of treatment.

I stepped into the massage room, glad to be finally alone. Was I truly alone? All of a sudden, I felt heat coming from the direction of my head. It was a cameraman. I sighed. I guess I would have to get used to it one more time. Following my massage, Terry and I were allowed to eat on the patio, even though we could not speak.

Awkwardly, I sat at a different table. There was no use asking why, so I decided to enjoy the silence. If you have ever heard of the different personalities people have, I am a SANGUINE, an extremely SOCIAL creature. I love people and making them feel comfortable. I knew almost all of the names of the cameramen, even though I could not converse with them a lot. SILENCE can be very difficult for me. Terry and I hated not being able to speak and eat with each other. However, I could sit uncomfortably, eating my salad, or bask in the quietness of my blessing. The trip had been a beautiful experience. I thought about how great Terry Clarkson was and how my life had been touched by our friendship. She was far more a gift than some opposing contestant on a TV reality show. I whispered a song of thanksgiving, and enjoyed the stillness of this rare moment.

It was time to depart for the airport. "Saying goodbye to Terry is just part of the journey and I don't think it's a goodbye forever," as I entered the car. The whole way to the airport, I sat in amazement of how incredible that week had been. The camera crew, the hotel staff and my new friend, Terry Clarkson, had all enriched my life beyond belief. My only wish was that Leo and the boys could have shared this experience with me. I couldn't even begin to imagine how their week had been; there was plenty to tell. As I exited the Houston airport, the producers totally caught me off guard! As usual, I was resigned to the fact that with NBC, anything could happen....

With new growth, are you willing to embrace change in your life?

Chapter 11

Stay in the Game

For some reason, upon exiting the airport, they BLIND FOLDED me. It had to remain on my head for the duration of my trip. I THOUGHT I was going home! I began to wonder as they talked about Dallas or San Antonio. I had just come off this beautiful resort experience, and once again, I'm feeling the effects of knowing that they own my every minute. Once again, I had to give them my total trust. I sat in the back seat, holding on to my purse. Finally, the driver said we had to stop so she could go to the restroom. To my surprise, they removed my blind fold. I started jumping up and down and saying, "I'm home, I'm home." They told me my family didn't know I was returning, so I was to walk in with a big smile and surprise them. As I walked to the apartment, I wondered if they had missed me as much as I missed them or what they were doing that very minute. I had been gone five days; I didn't know what to expect when I knocked on the door.

Looking back, I, Leo, felt that out of all the challenges they gave us, the pool party proved to be the hardest, causing us to come together as a team. We had to pick out the pool AND put it together. We had to invite ten guests. A pool, toys and food were chosen and purchased together as a TEAM. The boys tried to get some of the neighborhood kids to help us, but there was a message sent reminding us of the RULES of the game, stating we could not receive help; we had to do it all on our own. One of my friends told us later, that when he brought his son to the party, he saw how exhausted I was. He had even offered to help, but, of course, he couldn't. There were kids everywhere, jumping in and out of a pool that sat right out side the front door of our apartment. I thought pizza would be GREAT for a swimming party. We served junk food galore as kids hungrily ate everything we served. Nutrition has never been a big word in my vocabulary. Ree had just left Saturday morning, and by Sunday morning, we had gone shopping for an empty apartment AND bought a pool for an afternoon party! I didn't know if I was sinking or swimming. We had to fill up the pool by the time we left for church Sunday morning. We surprisingly made it to church early. I will never forget sitting in that church service, even though I still had a camera stuck in my face, thanking God I was in His house. Somehow, there was sanctuary there and it was very refreshing. As we loaded the van to go home, the producers were amazed at the message Joel preached that day. It completely tied into what we were going through with time management and the stress of everyday life. Pastor Joel shared about not getting caught up in the busyness of life. He said we should experience the refreshing waters of God's Presence. An entire scene of the message and actual service were included in the show, as only GOD could have orchestrated.

The most emotionally gripping time for me, was when I sat through a three-hour interview. They asked me lots of questions and had me talk. As I shared about missing my wife, I began to cry. By this time, I was emotionally raw and wrecked from this entire experience. One of the things I realized was that Ree and I are in close communication all the time, everyday. We are texting or calling each other daily. From the time they took her out of the picture, for several days, I had NO contact with her. It was very unsettling and unnerving for me. It really showed me how much God had made us one. I felt like a part of me was missing. It was almost like a death in the family. I began to value her in my life so much more. These feelings really came out in this interview. "I just really miss her. She is wonderful. I appreciate how much she does for the family; the things she adds to me and my life." After the show aired, people always talked about how my feelings for Ree touched their hearts the most. The thing I missed the most all week was her. It was not work or other things -- it was my wife. I, Ree, had no idea about the interview until commercials began airing him crying and hoping I would 'come home soon.' My mouth dropped. "I can't believe they are showing that interview on TV as a commercial," Leo said. My princess heart swelled at the thought of the world seeing my husband's love for me.

The final challenge of the game, was giving Mom a WELCOME HOME PARTY. I, Leo, was given a certain amount of money to spend. It wasn't a big challenge because we wanted to give her a party. But there were rules: we had to give her a summary of all the things we had been up to while she was gone. We also decorated the apartment floor to ceiling with balloons and streamers. We also bought her a cake. Ree was blown away when she walked through the doors. Our oldest son, Jon, wrote a song about all the things we had done. Later, the producers shared how they were amazed at the creativity of our party.

I, Ree, opened the door to shouts, balloons and noisemakers filling the air. Everyone was gathered in a huddle, screaming, "WELCOME HOME, MOM." Obviously, they DID know I was returning. Emotions soared, as we hugged and danced around the room. I had never had a party quite like this. Leo and I were always just glad to get through FIVE birthday parties a year; ours were definitely not celebrated to this extent. I felt APPRECIATED. It was a wonderful feeling to be missed and needed by everyone. After the big hurrahs, they presented me with a poster of pictures they had taken during the week. It was a collage of them modeling their new clothes, or eating at the Texas Chow Down competition. I could not believe the new clothes, linens and sheets they had bought without me. Leo totally surprised me; everything was beautiful. I didn't know he even knew how to shop, much less buy the beautiful bed spread he chose for our bed. Suddenly, Jon began playing a song he had written about their week. Speechless, I was totally amazed at my family's creativity and love for me. Working as a team, the show brought so many of their talents and abilities to light. "Honey," Leo shared later that night, "I wish I could tell you if I think we did well or not, but I have absolutely NO idea." The kids had gone to bed and we were quietly sharing about our week apart. I could not help but feel a little discouraged at his remarks, even though we both knew the producers were not allowed to tell or hint at the results. We prayed and drifted off to sleep. The game was officially over and no matter what; it was wonderful being home with my incredible family.

The next day was a bustle of activity. We got the kids off to school, knowing I had to pick them up by noon to fly to San Antonio for the Grand Finale. This was not easy since all five boys attended FIVE different schools. This took several hours, on top of packing and modeling clothes for the producers to choose which ones were television ready. The apartment was a mess after people returned all of our original clothes, linens and towels. We finally made it to the airport and flew back to San Antonio to face the opposing family for the final outcome of the game. Prior to walking into the elementary school, I was interviewed by our producer. "How do you think Leo did?" he asked. "I'm a little concerned about NUTRITION," I replied. As the cameras quit rolling, I said, "Freddy, whether we win or lose this game, I want you to know we've had the time of our lives. It has been absolutely AMAZING." He was thrilled to hear that because we had become friends and had bonded with the whole crew. We were then taken to an elementary school where Leo, the boys, Henry and the Clarkson girls sat behind desks in a Kindergarten room.

The moms stood in the front of the classroom, reading the judges' assessments. There were four categories: Parenting, Time Management, Nutrition and House Keeping. Every challenge our families faced, involved one or more of these four categories. They were written across a chalkboard. Terry and I stood nervously facing our families. Each time we finished reading our family's judgment, we flipped a card under that particular category, revealing our grade. Just like school, our grades could range from A to F. It was my turn to read the Parenting Category: "Mr. Beadle, one might think that your calm, unassuming personality would be trashed by five rambunctious boys. Quite the contrary, you are very involved and extremely well respected by them. Great job." I flipped the card over, revealing an A. I knew Leo would score well in Parenting. However, Nutrition was a different story! "On the one hand, you made sure they took their multi-vitamins everyday. Unfortunately, the whole story consists of junk food at the pool party, chili dogs for dinner and not nearly enough veggies all week. The Jolly Green Giant would not be happy!" Thanks to the vitamins, we ended up with a B-. It was a very close race with Henry leading in Nutrition and House Keeping, while Leo led in Parenting. It was time for the last category: Time Management. The air was thick with tension. "Mr. Beadle, you made it to church twenty minutes early. Your pool party was also ready with forty-five minutes to spare. You get an A+." There was a gasp in the air. Suddenly, we realized, by half a point, WE WON! I threw my arms in the air and ran to hug my family. We jumped up and down, crying and laughing.

A State Farm agent entered the room with a trophy the size of some of kids and a huge cardboard check for $25,000.00. (State Farm gave the prize money in the form of an educational savings account; we had the choice of using the money for college or spending it.) Following more shouting and hugging, we were escorted to another classroom. An attorney then reminded us that this prize money would be the down payment on a MILLION dollar fine if the press found out we had won before airing the show. We all looked at four-year-old Michael and took a deep breath! An interviewed followed. I was proud of my family as they all shared how wonderful the Clarkson family was and that the competition was very close. Wherever we went, the kids always spoke kindly of the Clarkson girls. They were and continue to be a great family. We were honored to compete against such fine people. We all did our best. We hated to say goodbye because we had become great friends.

After the Grand Finale, our family was invited to spend the night in the SAME resort I had been a few days before. We even got to stay in the same Presidential suite in which I had stayed. The kids were so excited. They ran around the hotel room in the fancy bathrobes they found in the closets as if they had never seen them before. They were able to hop on bikes outside, and ride all over the resort grounds. They enjoyed watching TV in the room, because during filming, TV, radio and cell phones were not allowed. They swam in the lazy river by the pool area, floating on big inner tubes. I was thrilled to be able to share my beautiful resort experience with my family. They flew us back home the next day. It suddenly dawned on me that we had flown four times back and forth to San Antonio; the kids had been there for the food competition a few days earlier. I had always wanted the kids to experience flying, and they certainly did.

Not knowing what they were going to throw at us next, for me, Ree, was the most difficult part of the show. That's kind of how life is, isn't it? We have to make the most of today. May, 2005, the 'windows of Heaven' opened up for the Beadles. Hopefully, viewers around the world saw and continue to see, that God loves the family. We are a reflection of Him. Life continued as normal, but on the inside, we changed. We were no longer victims, but as our Pastor Joel says every week, we are victors through Jesus Christ. Being somewhat of the visionary in our family, I kept wondering what God had for us later on.

Chapter 12

Moving Forward

August 9, 2005 arrived quicker than we anticipated. We had not been able to tell anyone we had won for ninety days. Twenty-five thousand dollars would be a drop in the bucket compared to the one MILLION dollar fine for spilling the beans. Almost one hundred guests watched the show with us at a nearby restaurant. Even though we knew the outcome, I, Ree, was still both nervous and excited. Three hundred hours of filming would be condensed into forty-five minutes of airtime. Commercials were running on a regular basis. NBC was anxious to introduce their summer reality shows; Biggest Loser or I Want to Be a Hilton. We could share what kinds of obstacles we encountered and the details of my spa trip, but not the final results.

Just like the discretion we used during the show, we were careful how we shared the details of our bankruptcy, with the children. We did not want to steal their ability to have an enjoyable childhood. We always made sure they knew we loved them and had their best interests at heart. To the degree we trusted God, was the degree to which we shared, whether it was with the kids, friends or outside family members. I shared a lot with close friends the first few years; talking things through has always been therapeutic for me. The more I surrendered to Christ, however, the less I had to voice the issues at hand. God wanted to heal us from the inside out, not the outside in.

There is a scripture that continues to minister to us as we go forward:

"Brethren, I count not myself to have apprehended: but this one thing I do, forgetting those things which are behind, and reaching forth unto those things which are before, I press toward the mark for the prize of the high calling of God in Christ Jesus." Philippians 3:13

We know that what we did, and continue to do, to move forward is just as important as what we did during the crisis. Taking risks is part of the journey. It is tempting to fear failure because of our past experiences, but that is not in our best interest. Some of you reading this book may have recently gone through an incredibly rough time in your lives. Don't let fear paralyze you from going forward. There are twice as many opportunities for the one you may have lost. Jesus could have been the only one to walk on water. Instead, he commanded Peter to get out of the boat. I can only imagine the thoughts running through his mind that dark night; probably a lot like mine. God told Moses that He would deliver the children of Israel because He loved them and because of the vows he had made to their forefathers. He never forgot what He had promised. We continue to remind God of His Word. Our Nation is in a severe economic crisis, but God is NOT limited by our financial state.

Leo and I were stunned when the bank offered our eighteen year old a CREDIT CARD with a $600.00 limit. At first, we hid it from Jon. One day, I asked him how much money he had in his account. "I don't know mom, BUT I have ALL my receipts." he eagerly replied. "Son, go get them." He emptied a shoebox full of receipts. "Jon, what does this spell?" I asked. "What do you mean, Mom?" "I mean this clump of receipts and no clue of your account balance. What does that mean?" "I don't know," he answered. "It spells b-a-n-k-r-u-p-t-c-y. Not knowing how much money we actually had to spend OR having money that we spent carelessly, is what ruined us financially. Do you want to repeat History?" We decided to give him the credit card as a test. Sure enough, $1000.00 had been charged before he knew what was happening. That was three years ago. Jon has paid off his car and credit card. He now UNDERSTANDS those years. We also made the decision to allow Jon to take his first semester off after graduating High School. We wanted him to work and SAVE money for college. The only one he could afford was a community college nearby. "All my friends are going AWAY to college. It's no fair!" he yelled. "I'm stuck behind, missing out on what they are probably experiencing." We knew he was not ready. A few years ago, a psychiatrist was talking about how many kids are not ready to go far away from home to college right after High School. They are exposed to stimulants, such as alcohol, that their brains are not biologically ready to handle. We wanted to make sure Jon was ready to handle life situations. It is amazing how well he did when he had to pay for college. He made grades he never made in High School and loved the small classroom atmosphere.

David graduates this year. We want our boys to grow into men that can support their families physically, spiritually and emotionally. We want them to be ALL God meant for them to be. We also teach them to TITHE, whether they make $10.00 or $1000.00. Their ten percent is sowing seed into our local church. This simple act of giving reminds us that life is not all about you or me; it is about the One who loved us and gave His life for us. We have also encouraged them to be involved in church ministry. It's tempting for them to play music for the sake of music. However, using their talents at Lakewood has caused them to mature in their FAITH as well as their talents.

Following the show in 2005, we focused on returning to our normal lives. Leo was ready to get back to what he loves doing: computers. Church, baseball, and school activities resumed. Our lease was up and it was time to look for a new home. Something I longed for, cried for, was finally becoming a reality. Leo and I, along with our realtor, walked into the home of our dreams. It even had

3 ½ BATHROOMS. It was so easy. They even offered a home complete with a washer/dryer, security AND sprinkler systems. We just moved in. The prize money enabled us to furnish our new castle with beautiful things. Leo and I walked into a furniture store and paid CASH for everything we needed. Swiping a debit card was definitely more invigorating than swiping a CREDIT card. We had Christmas before Christmas, as the truck delivered our new and beautiful treasures. Our lives were new, our home was new and our furniture was new. I love to entertain. It was so exciting to have friends visit from Louisiana, to discover all that had happened to us. The biggest blessing was that we had a place for my brother to live temporarily, following Hurricane Katrina. The miracles we encountered not only affected us, but those around us. God gives to us so we can give to others. He wants the world to know how much He loves mankind.

Jon is now a Music Intern at Lakewood Church. He is training in every area of worship ministry. It is amazing to watch him become all God has for him. Doors have opened widely for him, as he diligently seeks the Lord for his life to count for Him. All the years he played his guitar is paying off. He supports himself financially, as he works and attends the intern program. I believe the greatest lesson Jon has learned, is to have a RELATIONSHIP with Christ. It keeps his heart tender towards God. He says that when he gave God his agenda, the Lord replaced it with opportunities he never could have imagined. We refer to David as our 'drummer boy'.

He is co-captain of his High School's drum line. Last summer, he toured with Drum Corp International. His corps, the Troopers, competed with other corps all over the nation. He and his brothers enjoy participating in church worship activities. David also has his own band that plays at different functions around our area. They love to perform and write music. Chris is 16 and loves to sing. He has a great voice and is now trying his hand at writing lyrics. He is in the Lakewood youth choir and on the tennis team at school. Jeremy is 14 and loves to sing and play the violin. He continues to love and play baseball. The school programs have truly paid off for our sons. They have received instruction for reading music, as well as the disciplines involved in practicing and performing well. Mr. Michael is 9 years old and loves sports. He is showing a talent for drumming and singing. Again, church attendance and participation have been an excellent place for our sons to grow.

Our past has greatly affected our present situation. We do not look at money the same way we used to. First of all, we tithe no matter what. There was a time, early in our business, where we did not tithe on a regular basis. I want to strongly encourage those, especially who are walking through a crises, to tithe. We cannot AFFORD not to give. Food is created only when a seed is sown. A child is not created unless a seed is sown. Everything created, first began as a seed. God doesn't need our money. We need to trust Him when we give to our local church. Giving above and beyond can be a lot of fun, like supporting a child for World Vision, or church missionaries. I love our home, but it doesn't define me. No matter where we have lived, our family has and continues to be beautiful. We will always stay on a budget no matter what the income. I read a magazine article recently about a couple who wanted to live in a certain elite neighborhood. That was not enough, so they joined the nearby country club. Before long, their CLOTHES had to match their neighbors. As the credit cards mounted, their spending habits continued. The husband sadly wrote the article, sharing that even though they had to file bankruptcy, his wife's shopping had not lessened. They had even had to sell furniture, but they were hiding their losses from their friends lest they look LESS than everyone who they thought was IMPORTANT. I am thankful Leo and I got on the same page. We must become accountable to the same set of rules. It takes time to undo years of bad habits. There were four steps we took towards forgiveness we would like to share with you; We confessed and accepted full responsibility for our bankruptcy; we asked God to forgive us; We RECEIVED His grace; and Forgave OURSELVES. This process is good for any disappointment in our lives. Sometimes when I'm extra tired or feeling down, I glance at the beautiful scroll I received during the show: "Mom, you are the glue that holds the family together...." I smile, remembering what God did just for me. Suddenly, my heart beats a little faster, my pace quickens and my faith says, "Look out, there's more ahead!"

I, Leo, believe our lives flow in seasons like our natural seasons of winter, spring, summer and fall. There is a reason the earth has four seasons. Some give rest to the land and some require much work. Our lives cannot be set at just one speed or setting the whole time, or we would experience burn out. We have to have seasons of rest, toil, crises, transition, changes. The Word of God says we are being made in His image from glory to glory. I have heard people talking about mountain climbing. They say a climber cannot jump from mountain peak to mountain peak. He or she has to climb up the mountain, then down to the valley before climbing up to the next peak. There are cycles or seasons in our lives, a rhythm that is very important to the divine order in our lives. Today, we are in a different season than we were in the bankruptcy or the reality show. Through all the highs and lows, we must see the Hand of God. We must see His work at every turn of our lives. God's manifold wisdom does not just deal with us one way. We, as parents, do not merely deal with our children only one way. Even though there are times of strict discipline, there are times we give mercy and grace. The seasons of our lives bring us from place to place.

Today, I Ree, enjoy life. Raising five boys is difficult, tiring and wonderful all at the same time. Teaching a marriage class with Leo has helped us stay focused on what is really important: us. One of the highlights in my life is serving in our church choir. My mom now lives with us, so our home remains full. I have totally enjoyed writing this book, hoping others will have the courage to get up and dream again.

I, Leo, continue to work as a Systems Engineer and Software Developer. I love what I do. I have told the Lord that He can move me into any avenues He desires, because I never want to hinder God's plan in my life. We cannot be stuck wanting. If God wants me to be a Programmer the rest of my life, so be it. I'm open for whatever He has for me. Ree and I continue to teach a Young Married class at Lakewood Church. We enjoy teaching from our mistakes and triumphs, in hope they will grow together in their marriages and families. My final message to you would be this: do not assume you know what God wants you to do! Get it from Him! Trust His voice. Trust His leading. Do not step out without making well-informed, counseled decisions for your life. Do not make rash decisions that will drastically affect your family's future. For instance, do not up and quit your job one day because you thought you had heard from God and go home and inform your wife after the fact. Things like this are recipes for disaster. Remember, that just because the Holy Spirit speaks to you, it may not be for TODAY. Lastly, ENJOY the journey, whether you are in the valley or on the mountain top, STAY IN THE GAME.

I, Ree, picture Leo and me sharing our hearts with you, in the intimate surroundings of your home. As we sit at your table, maybe you are experiencing the difficulties of a bankruptcy or some other loss or disappointment. Maybe, you are fine and merely enjoyed reading about our reality show. Whatever the situation, I hope you have been strengthened and encouraged to MOVE FORWARD. I also hope you will consider us your new friends in Christ. Though we cannot physically see you, He does. No matter what the economy predicts God's Word NEVER changes. We would like to leave you with the same blessing our Pastor prays over us:

"May the Lord bless you and protect you, May the Lord smile on you and be gracious to you. May the Lord show you His favor and give you His peace."
(Numbers 6: 24-26)

This is our INHERITANCE; this is our REWARD.

APPENDIX

Chapter One:
1. Help!, performed by The Beatles, Written by John Lennon and Paul McCartney, page 12
2. Ruth 3:10-11, KJV, page 15

Chapter Two:
3. 2 Corinthians 12:9, KJV, page 36
4. Job 9:10-12a, NLT, page 37

Chapter Three:
5. Philippians 4:7, NLT, page 47
6. Job 3:25, KJV, page 50

Chapter Four:
1. What A Friend We Have In Jesus, Written by Joseph Scriver Music by Charles C. Converse, page 52
2. Luke 12:27, KJV, page 57
3. Don't Worry, Written by Rebecca St. James Music by Matt Bronleewe, page 57

Chapter Five:
4. Galatians 2:20, KJV, page 69
5. Romans 2:11, "For there is no respect of persons with God" KJV, page 70
6. Psalm 119:15, KJV, page 70
7. Psalm 46:1, KJV, page 72*

Chapter Six:
8. You Are Good, Words and Music by Israel Houghton, page 78
9. 1 Corinthians 11:24 * KJV, page 82

10. Psalm 91: 1-4 pages 83
11. Psalm 1:3-7, American KJV, page 84
12. Song of Solomon 2:4, KJV, page 85
13. Romans 8:25, KJV, page 86
14. Romans 5:5, the MSG, page 86
15. Deuteronomy 28:3, American KJV, page 87
16. Philippians 4:13, NKJV, age 87
17. Luke 1:17, KJV, page 88
18. Jeremiah 29:11, NLT, page 89
19. 2 Corinthians 4:17-18, American KJV, page 90
20. Mark 16:15, KJV, page 90

Chapter Seven:
21. Isaiah 41:18, KJV, page 98 *
22. Matthew 9:29, KJV, page 98

Chapter Eight:
23. Psalm 119:105, KJV, page 111
24. 1 Corinthians 2:9, NLT, page 120

Chapter Ten:
25. Henry David Thoreau, page 139
26. A real princess is always brave, page 146

Chapter Twelve:
27. Philippians 3:13, KJV, page 160
28. Numbers 6:24-26, NLT, page 168 *

"Streams In My Desert" by Rena Beadle appears on page 107.

www.ingramcontent.com/pod-product-compliance
Lightning Source LLC
Chambersburg PA
CBHW071926290426
44110CB00013B/1489